From Bethany to Gethsemane

[handwritten inscription] To Rev⁴ Guy ...

From Bethany
to Gethsemane

*Six crucial days in the last week of the Lord's
mortal life*

Peter Forbes

The Testimony
Birmingham
2022

First published 2022

© 2022 The Testimony

ISBN 978 0 85189 421 8 (print edition)

The Testimony acknowledges with grateful thanks the willing and expert help given by the staff of the Christadelphian Magazine and Publishing Association in the page-setting and printing of this book.

Printed and bound in the UK by
CMP (UK) Limited

Contents

Preface

This book began life in the distant past as a series of Bible School talks at Shawnigan Lake Bible School on Vancouver Island in Canada followed by further studies on the Monmouth Bible Campaign in the 1990s. Since then, much more study and various Bible Class papers later, the original work has been expanded and consolidated into book form.

The book does not aim to be exhaustive; instead, it has as its focus the provision of a calendar-framework for the events during the week leading up to the crucifixion of Jesus. Once events are 'calendared' in this way, the relationship between the events can be seen more clearly, giving rise to some valuable additional insights.

Mark's Gospel is taken as the basis for developing the calendar, as his account shows most clearly the days on which the events recorded took place. Arising from this approach, there are _apparent_ conflicts with the chronology of other Gospel records; but it is outside the scope of this study to attempt to resolve such issues.

I know that some will not agree with the precise order of the events as I have portrayed them. For example, there will be those who do not think that the meal in Bethany, where Jesus was anointed, took place two days before the Passover, when Jesus was crucified. My appeal on this, and other areas where there may not be agreement on chronology, is to reserve judgment until the evidence is presented, so that the exhortations can be drawn out.

Rather than simply studying the details of the events that took place during that crucial week in the Lord's life, the real aim of this work is to discover meaningful lessons for his disciples, for application in daily living.

Acknowledgements

There are many who have provided input into this study over the years – too many for me to name, in fact, especially as I would certainly forget to mention them all. The Father, however, is aware of all their valuable contributions.

In particular, though, I would like to thank my wife Norma for reading and commenting on many iterations of parts of this work; and I must also mention Brother Reg Carr, who has spent many hours, in difficult circumstances, making my original work more easily readable.

Peter L. Forbes
Loughborough
November 2021

Chapter 1:
By way of introduction

Studying the Gospels for ourselves

Whilst much has been written about the Gospel narratives and many Gospel parallels have been produced, the focus of this study will be to develop for ourselves tables, charts and parallels which will help us to understand the Gospel records better. In so doing, a deeper and more useful understanding of the life of Jesus and of the love of the Father will grow in our hearts. Bible study is not an end in itself: it is a means to an end. That end is to manifest the Father in our own lives. It is the entrance of God's word that gives light: "it giveth understanding unto the simple" (Ps. 119:130). Thus it is only to the extent to which we absorb the Scriptures that we will be able to manifest God's character. As Robert Roberts styled it,

> "Salvation depends upon the assimilation of the mind to the divine ideas, principles, and affections, exhibited in the Scriptures. This process … takes a lifetime … for its accomplishment. This is a work of slow development, and can only be achieved by the industrious application of the individual to the expression of [God's] mind in the Scriptures of truth" (Preface to *The Bible Companion*).

It follows, therefore, that the most valuable way to learn from Scripture is to examine it for ourselves.

This study reflects the writer's own, personal study, undertaken with the substantial help of others, through discussion. It is recommended that the reader takes the same approach. Review the Word of God for yourself. It may be that we think that when preparing talks, or beginning personal Bible study, that reading the works of others will give us a 'good start' or speed up our acquisition of knowledge. Whilst it may appear that this is a good method, especially for younger brethren and sisters, it is actually counterproductive. Following these methods fills our minds with the thoughts and analytical methods of others. Rather we should be filling our minds with the words and ideas of Scripture and developing a mind which mimics Scripture's way of developing ideas. This can only come from reading and thinking about Scripture. The works of others are helpful only to the extent to which they help us in that direction. We should not read the works of others simply to acquire information. The Father is not concerned with how much we know. Rather is He concerned with the degree to which we apply what we understand from His Word. Writing about giving, the Apostle Paul says: "For if there be first a willing mind, it is accepted according to that a man hath, and not according to that he hath not" (2 Cor. 8:12). The same basic principle should be applied in our analysis and application of the Scriptures. We should be like the Bereans, who "received the word with all readiness of mind, and searched the scriptures daily, whether those things were so" (Acts 17:11).

A basis for harmony

Critics assert that there are errors in the chronology of the Gospel records. Some claim that the differences are due to the Gospel writers' faulty memories about the details of the life of Jesus. We cannot accept such viewpoints as these. For Jesus himself promised his earliest disciples that when "the Spirit of truth, is come, he will guide you into all truth: for he shall not speak of himself; but whatsoever he shall hear, that shall he speak: and he will shew you things to come" (Jno. 16:13) To record the Gospels, the writers were not relying on memory, nor on instruction from other men. Instead, like the prophets of old, they were "moved by the Holy Spirit" (2 Pet. 1:21). Any differences between the Gospel records must be capable of satisfactory resolution.[1] It follows, therefore, that there are reasons for these apparent contradictions and discrepancies. These things are not preserved in the Scripture record in order to provide difficulties for Bible readers. Rather they highlight avenues for the research and discovery of themes and patterns which enrich our understanding of the mind of the Father. As Proverbs 25:2 explains, "It is the glory of God to conceal a thing: but the honour of kings is to search out a matter" (Prov. 25:2).

---

1 Writing about the resurrection of Jesus, and countering the Higher Critics (who conclude that the Gospel narratives cannot be reconciled with each other), Dr. John Wenham writes: "If ... it can be shown, at the point where the evangelists are thought to be most at sixes and sevens, that their accounts can be reconciled in detail and without strain, it suggests that much of the modern critical structure is on the wrong lines, and that the God who revealed himself in Jesus Christ saw to it that the church had a trustworthy record" (*The Easter Enigma*, Paternoster Press).

In relation to the chronology of the events narrated in the Gospels, we ought not to assume that it is possible to construct a detailed, over-arching chronological account. Instead, we should appreciate that each writer has his own inspired message, his own themes to develop; [2] and rather than imposing an overall chronology on the records, we might gain more from our study by viewing each record on its own, taking its chronology as the basis for the development of the narrative. An understanding of this narrative could then be enhanced by adding details from the other records, rather than by trying to resolve apparent discrepancies in the wider chronology. A more thorough understanding of the Gospels might benefit from producing four separate Gospel 'harmonies' – one for each of the Gospels. So, for example, in studying Matthew, we would use his chronology and ordering of events as our basis, adding data from the other records to fill out the record, and so on for each of the other Gospel accounts.

This study will use Mark's record as a basis for the chronological narrative, and will provide explanations for those places where events seem to be placed 'out of order', or in an order which appears to be at variance with that of any other Gospel(s). In order to gain the richness from the Word, we should be willing to think 'laterally' – that is, to consider that each Gospel writer has more to impart to us than simply a retelling of the events of Jesus' life. I suggest that each writer, in addition to setting out "a declaration of

---

2   We will see, when considering the meal in Bethany (recorded variously in Matthew 26, Mark 14 and John 12), that there is a clear reason why it appears that John places the meal on a different day from the two synoptic gospels.

those things which are most surely believed among us" (Lk. 1:1), has a range of important themes and patterns built into his account. Some of these themes, also, run across more than one record. From time to time, we will highlight such themes on the basis of the chronology of Gospel writers other than Mark.

Days and events

An example of one seeming contradiction relates to the way in which the entry of Jesus into Jerusalem and the cleansing of the temple are recorded. Both Matthew (21:9-14) and Luke (19:38-45) imply that Jesus entered the temple on the same day as his entry into Jerusalem on an ass. Only Mark informs us that the cleansing of the temple took place on the following day. On the day that Jesus arrived on the ass, he "entered into Jerusalem, and into the temple: and when he had looked round about upon all things, and now the eventide was come, he went out unto Bethany with the twelve" (Mk. 11:11). Mark records that the cleansing of the temple happened "on the morrow" (Mk. 11:12).

This study will allow Mark to provide the chronology of the week; and even where two other records *seem* to imply that Mark is incorrect, we will follow Mark's account. Neither Matthew nor Luke actually records that Jesus went into the temple on the same day as he entered Jerusalem on the ass. It is only Mark who puts a time-frame on the events. We can only infer from Matthew and Luke that the cleansing of the temple happened on the same day as the entry on the ass. If we had no other information, we might be justified in thinking that the two events happened on the same day. However, Mark adds specific details which Matthew and Luke do not provide.

This study will not, therefore, simply assume, just because there is no mention of particular days in the earlier part of Mark's Gospel, that the events recorded all took place on the same day. We shall merely assume that the events recorded covered a period of time, and we shall not try to break the events down into specific days. This last week of Jesus' life is recorded in a more detailed way in some of the records, with events being assigned to specified days. For example, Matthew and Luke record details in a way which is typical of the gospel narratives, while Mark provides additional data which makes it possible to situate the events in Matthew and Luke in their 'correct' place.

Implications for Inspiration

There are many who have difficulty with the idea that the Bible is the Word of God – that it was given by divine inspiration. This is despite the fact that the internal harmony of the Scriptures, and its thematic unity, provide powerful evidence as to its divine origin. [3] The Christadelphian *Declaration of the Truth revealed in the Bible* has no such reservations when it states:

> "The Bible is a revelation of God's purpose given through chosen men who were guided by His Spirit. It is therefore an infallible and authoritative expression of His will for man." [4]

---

3 J.J. Blunt's *Undesigned Coincidences* is a most helpful book in highlighting the veracity of the Scriptures by the examination of the internal harmony of the Bible.

4 *Declaration of the Truth revealed in the Bible* (Birmingham: The Christadelphian). First published in 1885, and still in print.

In writing details into a book to accentuate the credibility and perception of authenticity, an author may slightly disguise themes for the reader to discover. However, the Bible is in a different league. With the Gospel records we have four writers recounting the life of one man, his followers and his enemies. Each writer focuses differently on the same events and sometimes does not even mention an event recorded in up to three of the other accounts. Woven into each record are themes which rely on the reader's understanding of the Old Testament concept of Messiah in a way which differs from the way that Messiah was viewed by his contemporaries. The Gospel accounts present Messiah as a man who would overcome sin and who, in so doing, would be crucified and rise again from the dead. But his contemporaries viewed Messiah as a conquering warrior. Additionally, themes and echoes from the lives of earlier Old Testament characters are woven into each record. In some cases, these themes – which are not even necessary to an understanding of the narrative – are seen across the writing of more than one of the writers. How can this be explained? It is not to be expected that four secular historians or biographers writing about the same group of people or events in history would build their writings in such a way. We would not expect to find a detailed, but concealed, theme in one writer to be seen developed in another writer. Yet this is exactly what we find in the Gospel narratives. These details, which we will return to time and again, force the conclusion that the Gospel writers wrote under the inspiration of God. Their narratives are not simply the recollections of men who knew Jesus; nor are they just accurate accounts of his life. Rather they are the mind of the Father on the matter.

Such details serve to confirm and support the belief in the verbal inspiration of Scripture. They can counter the arguments of Bible critics about the veracity and reliability of the Scriptures. But above all, the wonder of the revelation of the Father's mind ought to engender in us a love, awe and respect for God's Word. Well might we say, with the Psalmist, "Open Thou mine eyes, that I may behold wondrous things out of Thy law" (Ps. 119:18); for unless we believe that there are such "wondrous things" in the Word of God we will never see them, and our lives in Christ will be all the poorer for it.

Chapter 2:
Six days – an overview

A summary of the week

This study reviews the events of that part of the last week of Jesus' mortal life from his arrival in Bethany, six days before the Passover, until his arrest in the garden of Gethsemane.

The following summary of the related Gospel passages for each of these last six days is used as the basis for the rest of the study, and should provide a useful ready reference for noting the parallel passages relevant to each day.

Six days before the Passover

Matthew	Mark	Luke	John
			12:1

Five days before the Passover

Matthew	Mark	Luke	John
21:1-11	11:1-10	19:29-44	12:12-19

Four days before the Passover

Matthew	Mark	Luke	John
21:18-19	11:11-18	19:45-48	

Three days before the Passover

Matthew	Mark	Luke	John
21:20–25:46	11:20–13:37	20:1–21:36	12:19-50

Two days before the Passover

Matthew	Mark	Luke	John
26:1-16	14:1-11	22:1-3	12:2-8

One day before the Passover

Matthew	Mark	Luke	John
26:17-56	14:12-52	22:7-53	13:1-18-12

A more detailed summary

The more detailed summary given below shows the days before the Passover and the events recorded in the Gospels that took place on each day. The parallel accounts of the same event in each Gospel will help to clarify the details of the events of the week. The time of day when the event took place and the location of the event are also included where known. (It is not possible, with some of the events, to be certain exactly when and where a particular event took place; but in such cases an 'educated guess' has been made.)

The objective of these summaries is to provide a working framework for the events of the week that will enhance our studies and make it easier for us to visualise the flow of events.

Six days before the Passover

Events	Matthew	Mark	Luke	John	Time	Place
Jesus arrives in Bethany				12:1	PM	Bethany

Five days before the Passover

Events	Matthew	Mark	Luke	John	Time	Place
Triumphal entry into Jerusalem	21:1-11	11:1-10	19:29-44	12:12-19	AM	Outside Jerusalem
Jesus weeps over Jerusalem			19:41			
Jesus looks round		11:11				Temple
Returns to Bethany with disciples		11:11			Late PM	Bethany

Four days before the Passover

Events	Matthew	Mark	Luke	John	Time	Place
Jesus curses the barren fig tree	21:18-19	11:11-18			AM	Mt. of Olives
Cleansing of the Temple	21:12-13	11:15-18	19:45-48			Temple
Some Greeks desire to see Jesus				12:20-36		Temple
Jesus responds to the unbelief of the crowd				12:37-50		Temple

Events	Matthew	Mark	Luke	John	Time	Place
Return to Bethany		11:19			Late PM	Bethany

Three days before the Passover

Events	Matthew	Mark	Luke	John	Time	Place
Disciples see the withered fig tree	21:18-22	11:20-26			AM	Mt. of Olives
Priests question Jesus' authority	21:23-27	11:27-33	20:1-8			Temple
Which son did his father's will?	21:28-32					Temple
Parable of the vineyard	21:33-46	12:1-12	20:9-19			Temple
Parable of the wedding banquet	22:1-14					Temple
Paying taxes to Caesar	22:15-22	12:13-17	20:20-26			Temple
Sadducees' question about the resurrection	22:23-33	12:18-27	20:27-40			Temple
Which is the great commandment?	22:35-40					Temple
Which is the first commandment?		12:28-34				Temple
Whose son is Christ?	22:41-46	12:35-37	20:41-44			Temple
We prevail nothing against him				12:19		

Events	Matthew	Mark	Luke	John	Time	Place
Greeks come to see Jesus				12:20-26		
Now is my soul troubled				12:27-28		
A voice as thunder				12:28		
Jesus speaks to the people				12:30-36		
But though he had done so many miracles …				12:37-41		
Nevertheless some rulers believed				12:42-43		
A final appeal				12:44-50		
Woe unto you … hypocrites	23:1-39	12:38-40	20:45-47			Temple
The poor widow's gift		12:41-44	21:1-4		Late PM?	Treasury
The Olivet prophecy	24:1-36	13:1-32	21:5-36		Late PM	Mt. of Olives
Watch, days of Noah	24:37-51					Mt. of Olives
Ten virgins	25:1-13					Mt. of Olives
Man travelling into a far country	25:14-31	13:33-37				Mt. of Olives
Sheep, goats and judgment	25:31-46					Mt. of Olives

Two days before the Passover

Events	Matthew	Mark	Luke	John	Time	Place
Sanhedrin plot to kill Jesus	26:1-5	14:1-2	22:1-2		AM	Palace of high priest?
The meal in Bethany	26:6-13	14:3-9		12:2-3	Eve	Bethany
Mary anoints Jesus for his burial	26:6-13	14:3-9		12:2-8	Eve	Bethany
Judas agrees to betray Jesus	26:14-16	14:10-11	22:3-6			Temple?

One day before the Passover

Events	Matthew	Mark	Luke	John	Time	Place
Preparation for the Passover meal	26:17-20	14:12-17	22:7-14		AM	Jerusalem
Disciples strive about "who is the greatest?"			22:24-30		Eve	Upper room
Jesus washes the disciples' feet				13:1-20		Upper room
Identification of Jesus' betrayer	26:21-25	14:18-21	22:21-23	13:21-30		Upper room
Memorial meal instituted	26:26-29	14:22-25	22:15-20			Upper room
Judas leaves				13:30		Upper room
A new commandment I give you				13:31-35		Upper room

Events	Matthew	Mark	Luke	John	Time	Place
Prediction of Peter's denial	26:31-35	14:27-31	22:31-38	13:36-38		Upper room
Discourses in the Upper Room				14:1-31		Upper room
Then they sang a hymn	26:30	14:26				Upper room
Then they leave the Upper Room				14:31		On the way to Kidron
Abide in me				Chap. 15		On the way to Kidron
I go my way				Chap. 16		On the way to Kidron
Jesus lifted up his eyes to heaven				Chap. 17		On the way to Kidron
Jesus prays in Gethsemane	26:36-46	14:26-42	22:39-46		Night	Geth-semane
Jesus betrayed, arrested, forsaken	26:47-56	14:43-52	22:47-53	18:2-12		Geth-semane

'The evening and the morning': the Jewish day

In order to understand better the time-periods and events recorded in the Gospels we need to appreciate that the Jewish way of recording days differs from the Western approach. In the West our 'day' starts at midnight, whereas the Jewish 'day' starts in the evening. This is seen in the way in which the days of Creation are spoken of in Genesis: "... and the evening and the morning were the (nth) day" (Gen. 1:5, 8, 13, 19, 23, 31), where (nth) stands for a particular day of Creation.

In the Gospels, therefore, the 'day' commences at 6pm, which in Israel is roughly sunset. Thus, when Jesus arrived in Bethany "six days before the Passover" (Jno. 12:1), we know this means that he arrived in Bethany _before_ 6pm, which is reasonable, since travelling in the dark would be avoided wherever possible. The "next day" (Jno. 12:12), when Jesus entered into Jerusalem on the colt, was therefore _five_ days before the Passover, as the twelve hours of the night had passed and the daylight hours had just begun.

This Jewish method of reckoning the day is the only method that allows for all the details in the last week of Jesus' life to be fitted together, as can be seen from the table at the end of this study.

Places in the last week of Jesus' mortal life

The map opposite shows only a small part of the land of Israel; but it provides a guide to the location of the places mentioned in the last week of Jesus' life. Jericho and Ephraim are included because Jesus made his way from a city called Ephraim via Jericho to Bethany on his way up to his last Passover. Emmaus is the village to which the two were walking after Jesus' resurrection. The Mount of Olives is North and East of Bethany. Bethany is on the lower slopes of the Mount of Olives.

A calendar of events and parallel passages

The four Gospels provide a detailed diary of the events of the last week of Jesus' life that culminated in the Crucifixion.

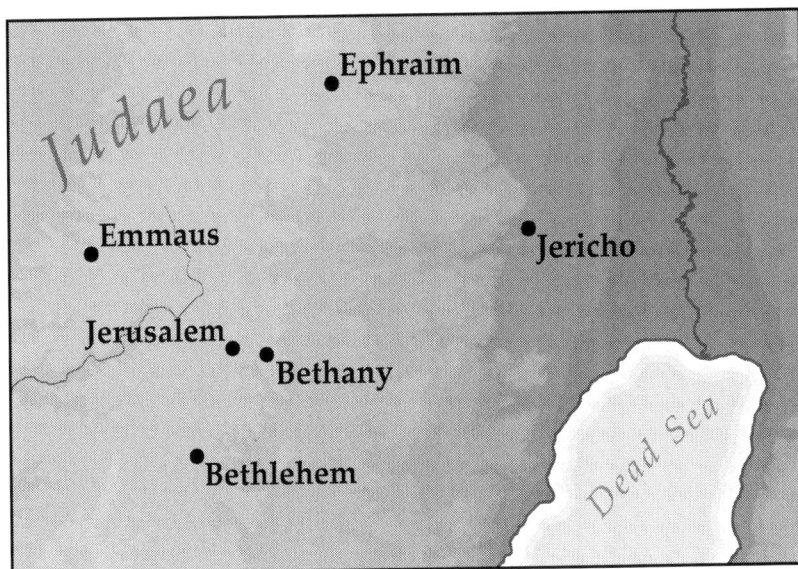

Mark's record provides a calendar of the days from Jesus' arrival in Bethany to the evening when Jesus was taken prisoner. We know that Mark 11:1 is five days before the Passover because it is the day after Jesus arrived in Bethany (we know he arrived "six days before the Passover" – Jno. 12:1).

So here is the calendar showing the relevant parallel passages:

Mark	Matthew	Luke	John	Day before Passover
			12:1	6
11:1	21:1	19:29	12:12	5
11:12	21:8	19:45		4
11:20	21:20	20:1		3
14:1	26:2	22:1		2

Mark	Matthew	Luke	John	Day before Passover
14:12	26:17	22:7	13:1	1

By piecing together the four accounts and placing them within the timeframe of the last week we are better able to understand what happened during those days.

The following pages provide an outline of that week, placing the four Gospel records together and setting the events into the day on which they happened. Thus, it is possible to see at a glance which passages provide information about the events of the week and on which days those events took place. The notes that follow are an expansion of the tables given above. [1]

Mark's Gospel: the basis

The "six days before the Passover" of John 12:1 provides the fixed and certain starting point for the events that are to follow. The "next day" mentioned in John (12:12) must be five days before the Passover. This answers to Mark 11:1. The use in Mark 11:12 of "on the morrow" and 11:20 "in the morning" indicates the careful ordering that Mark, through the Spirit, provides. This analysis is confirmed when the next day that Mark mentions (14:1) is "two days before the Passover". This detail is confirmed by Matthew (26:2) where Jesus told his disciples, "Ye know that after two days ...". This is the detailed, confirmed and cross-checked rationale for the table immediately above.

---

1   The location of the events has been left off the tables in the remainder of the study in the interests of simplicity.

Using the gospel of Mark as the basis for what follows, it is possible, with relative certainty, to slot the other Gospel records into this assured framework, and thereby to establish clearly what happened on each of the days of the week that culminated in the crucifixion of Jesus.

A note on distribution

Before moving on to review the week in detail some comments about the distribution of information are in order. The table above shows that Scripture does not devote similar amounts of space to each of the six days. It will also be noticed that John is the only record which does not provide enough data to allow any differentiation of the days between the 'triumphal entry' and the evening of the 'last supper'.

The tables that follow show, in the left-hand column, a specific event. The next four columns show the related passages in the Gospels and the final column shows the time of the day when the event took place. This makes it possible, at a glance, to see what took place on each day and to see the related passages of Scripture at the same time.

Events	Matthew	Mark	Luke	John	Time
Jesus arrives in Bethany				12:1	PM

Six days before

Six days before the Passover Jesus arrives with his disciples in Bethany in the afternoon (Jno. 12:1).

We note, first, how the arrival in Bethany fits into John's Gospel account. None of the other Gospel writers even mentions the arrival in Bethany. Their focus is on the entry into Jerusalem on the next morning (Mt. 21:1; Mk. 11:1; Lk. 19:29).

The last detailed event of John's Gospel is the raising of Lazarus at Bethany (Jno. 11:1-44). It was this event that caused the Pharisees to take "counsel together for to put him (Jesus) to death" (11:53). The effect of this discussion was that "Jesus therefore walked no more openly among the Jews; but went thence unto a country near to the wilderness, into a city called Ephraim, and there continued with his disciples" (11:54). After this, John records that "the Jews' Passover was nigh at hand" (11:55), thus skipping over whatever happened in the "city called Ephraim".

None of the other Gospels records anything directly about the time that Jesus was in "Ephraim". There is, however, a section in Luke (from chapter 10 to 18:14) that is not found in any other record. Luke follows this with a short section (18:15 to 19:28) which is matched in the other synoptic Gospels; and this is followed by the comment: "And it came to pass, when he was come nigh to Bethphage and Bethany" (Lk. 19:29), which can be taken to match the day after the arrival in Bethany of John 12:1. Luke 10:38-42 mentions Martha and her sister Mary and seems to speak of a time when Jesus was in Bethany. [2] The fact that "Martha was cumbered about much serving" (10:40) may

---

2 The evidence that this is one and the same time as John 11 is circumstantial. However, the presence of the same two sisters in both records may be an indication that the events are related in time and place.

be a consequence of the number of visitors to the house at the time of Lazarus' death. We know that Jesus left Bethany and went to 'Ephraim' _after_ raising Lazarus (Jno. 11:54); therefore, it is reasonable to conclude that the section of Luke from chapter 11 to 18:14 relates to events that took place while Jesus was in 'Ephraim'. So the section in Luke is situated in the interval between the raising of Lazarus and the arrival in Bethany, six days before the Passover.

Whereas John then records the anointing of Jesus in Bethany in the same breath, so to speak, as "six days before the Passover" (Jno. 12:2), that event did not actually occur until two days before the Passover (Mt. 26:2,6; Mk. 14:1). John relates the details of the meal in Bethany at this point in the record because the meal is thematically linked with the raising of Lazarus, recorded in John 11:1-44. The meal in Bethany of which John 12 speaks was a celebratory meal to commemorate the raising of Lazarus. Further study will show that the meal in the upper room (Jno. 13–14:31) also has a number of powerful links with the meal at Bethany. These links will be investigated when we look at the day which was "two days before the Passover". At that time, we will also consider the details which demonstrate that the meal in Bethany did actually take place two, and not six, days before the Passover. It will become clear at that point that John has little to say about the events of days 5 to 2 before the Passover. His focus is on the meal in Bethany, its relationship to the raising of Lazarus, the meal in the upper room and subsequent events.

This should alert us to the fact that whilst Matthew, Mark and Luke take a fairly systematic chronological journey through the events of the last week, John is more thematic in the things he records. If only for this reason, therefore, it would be unwise to base a chronology of the last week of Jesus' life on John's Gospel. Furthermore, if we find apparent discrepancies between John and the other records, we should not assume that John is either speaking of a different event or that there is some error in one or more of the other records.

This consideration should be taken into account when examining any part of the Gospel records. Each writer has, by the Spirit, specific points to make; and the record is structured to highlight these features. If we focus on attempting to reconcile apparent contradictions rather than on the detail in the writers' distinctive aims and themes, we may well miss the richness of the message.

By telling us that Jesus was in Bethany "six days before the Passover", John has provided a specific day from which we can commence our chronology for the week. As will be seen, it is John, in fact, who provides the starting point for this week and therefore acts as the lynch pin for identifying the day of the Crucifixion, as well as for showing the sense in which Jesus was in the tomb for "three days and nights".

Chapter 3:
Five days before the Passover

Events	Matthew	Mark	Luke	John	Time
Triumphal entry into Jerusalem	21:1-11[1]	11:1-10	19:29-44	12:12-19	AM
Jesus weeps over Jerusalem			19:41		AM
Jesus looks round		11:11			
Returns to Bethany with disciples	21:17[7]	11:11			Late PM

After the digression of John 12:2-11, John tells us that "on the next day" (Jno. 12:12) Jesus went up to Jerusalem. We

---

1   It will be noticed that Matthew 21:12-16 are not included in this section of the week. Those verses, which speak of the casting out of the money changers, are a digression and relate to events which took place on the next day. This can be seen by comparing the order of events with Mark. We will return to this point later in the study.

can therefore be certain that this day is actually five days before the Passover.

Five days before the Passover we have what is usually called the 'triumphal entry into Jerusalem'. There is very little recorded about the events of this fifth day before the Passover. All the Gospels record the entry into Jerusalem and little else. We must conclude, therefore, that it is a very significant incident. Mark summarises the activities of the day by saying, "Jesus entered into Jerusalem, and into the temple: and when he had looked round about upon all things, and now the eventide was come, he went out unto Bethany with the twelve" (Mk. 11:11). So all we know of the day is the entry into Jerusalem, a visit to the temple where Jesus "looked round", and the return to Bethany in the late afternoon.

The events recorded would hardly fill a whole day. The couple of miles journey from Bethany to Jerusalem, even allowing for time to secure the use of the animals and the thronging of the people, would not take more than two hours. If Jesus left Bethany at about 8am, he would have been in the temple precinct by about 10.15am. Mark then records that Jesus "looked round" (11:11), but immediately says that "eventide was come". We are told nothing of the events of the day between Jesus entering the temple and leaving to return to Bethany. Reflecting on the timescale suggests that the entry into the city and the acclamation of the people was the focus of the day.

The triumphal entry into Jerusalem is one of the few events in Scripture recorded in all four Gospels. This should alert us to the great significance of this event in the life of Jesus. As if to reinforce this, it is the only event of that day that is recorded in any detail. From a consideration of the four

Gospel records we learn that Jesus, to the acclamation of his disciples (Lk. 19:37) and the people (Jno. 12:12-13), travelled up to Jerusalem. As he neared the city he wept over it (Lk. 19:41) and spoke of the judgment that was to come upon it (Lk. 19:42-44). He entered Jerusalem, went into the temple, looked round, and subsequently returned to Bethany.

The descent of the Mount of Olives

Describing Jesus' journey towards Jerusalem, Luke says, "And when he was come nigh, even now at the descent of the Mount of Olives" (Lk. 19:37). In describing Jesus' location in this way, Luke introduces the first of many echoes of language and events from the life of David. We will see this time and again. [2] On this occasion the echo is to the time when David was fleeing from Absalom. Of this time we read that "David went up by the ascent of mount Olivet" (2 Sam. 15:30). The contrasts and similarities between the two events are noted here:

Luke 19 event	2 Samuel 15 event
v. 37 Descent	v. 30 Ascent
v. 37 Disciples with Jesus	vv. 16-17 Followers with David
vv. 37-38 People rejoicing	v. 23 People weeping

So we see one king travelling towards Jerusalem to the acclaim of the people, whereas his father David flees from the city amidst anguish and grief among the people. Just as those who were with David did not then know the eventual outcome for David, so those rejoicing over Jesus did not

---

2   Some of these echoes are tabulated in Appendix 2, "Bible echoes: David's flight from Absalom" on page 224.

know what would befall him in the city in the next few days. Indeed, the evidence indicates that they thought that he would, in fulfilment of their expectations of Messiah, throw out the Romans and take control of the nation. But instead, Jesus threw out the religious leaders and took control of his own death.

There is a further contrast between David and Jesus in these events. For David did not know what was going to happen to him. He had already told Zadok, "if I shall find favour in the eyes of the LORD, He will bring me again, and shew me both it, and His habitation: But if He thus say, I have no delight in thee; behold, here am I, let Him do to me as seemeth good unto Him" (2 Sam. 15:25-26). By contrast, Jesus had previously talked with Moses and Elijah about "his decease [3] which he should accomplish at Jerusalem" (Lk. 9:31); and he had told his disciples, "Behold, we go up to Jerusalem; and the Son of man shall be delivered unto the chief priests, and unto the scribes; and they shall condemn him to death, and shall deliver him to the Gentiles" (Mk. 10:33). David fled from Jerusalem lest Absalom should "smite the city with the edge of the sword" (2 Sam. 15:14). But because Jesus was rejected by the people, he had to warn them that they would "fall by the edge of the sword" (Lk. 21:24). It was this (fore)knowledge that caused Jesus to weep over the city as it came into view.

Human emotions

It is worth considering the contrasting human emotions that were being experienced at that time. The disciples and others

---

3 The Greek word for "decease" means 'exodus', and clearly speaks of the Exodus from Egypt. The same word is translated "departing" in Hebrews 11:22, where Joseph spoke of the Exodus before he died.

walking with Jesus to Jerusalem evidently had expectations which made them joyful. Clearly, as it was Passover time, emotions were high anyway. Passover reminded Israel of their deliverance from bondage in Egypt; and they had been commanded to perpetuate this understanding of the Passover: "And it shall be when thy son asketh thee in time to come, saying, What is this? that thou shalt say unto him, By strength of hand the LORD brought us out from Egypt, from the house of bondage" (Ex. 13:14). At the time of Jesus' birth there were those in Israel "waiting for the consolation of Israel" (Lk. 2:25); and many of the people thought that Jesus was "that prophet" (Jno. 6:14) – clearly a reference to the words of Moses in Deuteronomy 18:15 ("The LORD thy God will raise up unto thee a Prophet from the midst of thee, of thy brethren, like unto me; unto him ye shall hearken"). Even Pilate seemed to have in mind some notion of redemption associated with Passover when he said to the Jews assembled before him, "ye have a custom, that I should release unto you one at the Passover" (Jno. 18:39). The people had, for over three years, seen Jesus' miracles and heard his preaching. The seventy weeks prophecy had run its course. The time was ripe for Israel's redeemer to appear. A few days later there were those who were willing to say to a stranger, "But we trusted that it had been he which should have redeemed Israel" (Lk. 24:21). Yet all these hopes were based on nationalism. Many, no doubt, would have been willing to join an armed uprising against the Romans with Jesus as their captain and leader. Such is the short-sighted folly of mankind, and of nationalists in particular.

On the other hand, Jesus had a very different perspective. He would later tell Pilate, "My kingdom is not of this world" (Jno. 18:36). Jesus understood that deliverance from bondage to Rome would only be a short-term solution for the problems of the people. After all, every one of those who were delivered from Egypt in the days of Moses died eventually. That deliverance was short-lived. Jesus had already told those who said, "We be Abraham's seed, and were never in bondage to any man" (Jno. 8:33) that "whosoever committeth sin is the servant of sin" (Jno. 8:38). Because Jesus' focus was on deliverance from sin and death, his approach was different from a nationalistic leader bent on a military campaign. He was certainly involved in a tremendous battle, but it was a personal one. He "was in all points tempted like as are we" (Heb. 4:15), yet he was "without sin". His battle was a battle with his human nature. The deliverance he was working to achieve could only be achieved if he was able to rule his own life and actions. In this respect, the contrast between the nationalist seeking to overcome the occupying power and Jesus striving to overcome his own temptations to sin provides a powerful challenge to us.

Lowly, riding upon an ass

Matthew, Mark and Luke all describe the method by which the animal that Jesus rode into Jerusalem was obtained. The simple answer "the Lord hath need" (Mt. 21:3; Mk. 11:3; Lk. 19:31) was sufficient to satisfy the owner of the animal(s). So the disciples returned to Jesus with the animal(s), and it is left to Matthew to inform us that Scripture is being fulfilled in the events that were to follow, saying: "All this was done, that it might be fulfilled which was spoken by the prophet, saying, Tell ye the daughter of Sion, Behold, thy King cometh unto thee, meek, and sitting upon an ass, and a colt the foal of an ass" (Mt. 21:4-5). The Scripture being fulfilled is Zechariah 9:9: "Rejoice greatly, O daughter of Zion; shout, O daughter of Jerusalem: behold, thy King cometh unto thee: he is just, and having salvation; lowly, and riding upon an ass, and upon a colt the foal of an ass".

An examination of the context of Zechariah 9 shows that the prophet is speaking about a time when Israel's enemies will be overthrown. This will be because "the eyes of man, as of all the tribes of Israel, shall be toward the LORD" (9:1). Additionally, Israel was no longer to be oppressed because the LORD would be encamped around Jerusalem (9:8). It is against the background of a peaceful Jerusalem that was not trodden down that the king was to come (9:9), saying that he shall "speak peace unto the heathen" (9:10). "His dominion shall be from sea even to sea and from the river even to the ends of the earth" (9:10).

These words of Zechariah are a reminder of a Psalm which speaks of Messiah. Zechariah teaches us that the one he speaks of is the king who "shall have dominion also from sea to sea, and from the river unto the ends of the earth" (Ps. 72:8). By drawing our attention to Zechariah 9:9, Matthew clearly marks Jesus out as Messiah – but not as a warrior who will fight against the Roman occupying force. Instead, Matthew presents Jesus as one who is going to release prisoners: "As for thee also, by the blood of thy covenant I have sent forth thy prisoners out of the pit wherein is no water" (Zech. 9:11). This would be the culmination of the work of Jesus, who said: "Woman, thou art loosed from thine infirmity" (Lk. 13:1). The very miracles that Jesus performed were the evidence that he also had power to forgive sins, for he himself linked the performing of his miracles with the forgiveness of sins: "But that ye may know that the Son of man hath power on earth to forgive sins, (then saith he to the sick of the palsy,) Arise, take up thy bed, and go unto thine house" (Mt. 9:6). This work of deliverance from sin and death would become effective, not through removing the Romans by force, but by submitting to the will of his Father. All of this is to be seen in the prophecy which Matthew quotes from Zechariah 9.

It is worth comparing the words of Matthew with the words of Zechariah. In so doing it becomes clear that there are some differences; and these differences serve to place an important emphasis on certain key words of the prophet. In the table below the *words in italic type* are common to both passages. [4]

Zechariah 9:9	Matthew 21:5
"Rejoice greatly, O *daughter of Zion*; shout, O daughter of Jerusalem: *behold, thy King cometh unto thee*: he is just, and having salvation; *lowly, and riding upon an ass, and upon a colt the foal of an ass*"	"Tell ye the *daughter of Sion, Behold, thy King cometh unto thee, meek, and sitting upon an ass, and a colt the foal of an ass*"

Matthew omits the words "he is just, and having salvation". The name 'Jesus' means 'God is salvation' or 'God saves', and as Jesus nears the city the people cry out for salvation, saying "Hosanna" (Mt. 21:9, etc.), which means "Save now", quoting Psalm 118:25. The common people understood their need for salvation; but their expectations were short sighted. They only saw salvation as deliverance from the occupying Romans; but Jesus had a far greater objective.

---

4   There are various places in Scripture where we are told that an earlier passage is being quoted but the words do not match exactly. This gives an insight into how quotation works in the Bible. The meaning of the section quoted is preserved but not necessarily the precise words. This allows for the later inspired writer to explain/expound the passage quoted.

Whereas there was a ground swell of expectation that Jesus would save both land and people from the Romans, the biblical prophecies about the coming of Messiah promised not a deliverance from a human power, but deliverance from sin and death. This misunderstanding on the part of the common people helps to explain their apparently fickle change of mind when, in another five days, they would be crying out "Crucify him, crucify him" (Lk. 23:21). The people who welcomed Jesus as he entered the city at the beginning of the week became disillusioned because their own expectations had not been met. This is why they were susceptible to being manipulated by the chief priests.

In this there is a warning for us. We have expectations which we are sure are based on Scripture. We know for sure that Jesus will return to re-establish the Kingdom of God with Jerusalem as its capital. But it is likely that we do not know or understand the precise ordering and details of events leading up to the Lord's return. We must take care, therefore, to ensure that certain knowledge and uncertain details are not confused. Our expectations must be based on the clear teaching of Scripture.

Blessed is he that cometh in the name of the LORD

Psalms 113–118 (the Hallel psalms) are psalms of praise that were sung at feast times such as Passover.

Passover celebrated the deliverance from Egypt, and the Jewish people were living in expectation of deliverance from the Romans. They saw Jesus as the Messiah who would effect that deliverance; and so it is hardly surprising that they should call out some of the words of Psalm 118, "Hosanna, blessed is the king of Israel that cometh in the name of the LORD" (Jno. 12:13). In speaking of salvation and deliverance, Psalm 118 lent itself to being used at Passover time to express the expectations of the people at this highly charged season in their religious calendar.

Psalm 118 is referred to extensively in the last week of the life of Jesus. It is used by the common people when Jesus arrives on the colt ("the foal of an ass") at the beginning of the week. It is also used two days later by Jesus to confound the Jewish leaders. And the words are, so to speak, put into the mouths of those same critics by Jesus in his last words to them. The table below shows the links between Psalm 118 and the work of Jesus as Messiah in Jerusalem just before his final Passover.

Psalm 118	Language	New Testament
v. 25	"Save now" / "Hosanna"	Matthew 21:9; Mark 11:9; John 12:13
v. 26	"Blessed is he that cometh in the name of the LORD"	Matthew 21:9; Mark 11:9; Luke 19:38; John 12:13
v. 22-23	"The stone which the builders rejected the same is become the head of the corner. This is the LORD's doing and it is marvellous in our eyes"	Matthew 21:42; Mark 12:10-11; Luke 20:17
v. 26	"Blessed is he that cometh in the name of the LORD"	Matthew 23:39

Hosanna

Matthew, Mark and John all record that the people cried "Hosanna'. The Greek word *hosanna* (which is only ever translated "Hosanna") is of Hebrew origin and is a composite of two Hebrew words, *yasha* and *na*. The Hebrew word *yasha* is translated variously in the Authorised Version as:

'save' (149 times); 'saviour' (15); 'deliver' (13); 'help' (12); 'preserved' (5); 'salvation' (3); 'avenging' (2); 'at all' (1); 'avenged' (1); 'defend' (1); 'rescue' (1); 'safe' (1); 'victory' (1).

Of the word's 205 occurrences, therefore, more than 94% of its uses relate to salvation.

The Hebrew word *na* is commonly translated in the AV as "beseech" or "pray". So we can safely conclude that "Hosanna" means 'Please save us (now)'. This answers exactly to the Psalm, where we find "Save now, I beseech thee" (Ps. 118:25). The people were quoting the Psalm and looking to Jesus as the one who would save them.

We do not know whether the people sang the whole of the Psalm or only parts of it – the Spirit merely records some words that the people and the disciples sang. So what can we conclude from the parts of the Psalm that we know they sang?

Each of the four Gospels presents a slightly different account of what was said.

- *Matthew 21:9* – "And the multitudes that went before, and that followed, cried, saying, Hosanna to the son of David: Blessed (is) he that cometh in the name of the LORD; Hosanna in the highest"

- *Mark 11:9-10* – "And they that went before, and they that followed, cried, saying, Hosanna; Blessed (is) he that cometh in the name of the LORD: Blessed (be) the kingdom of our father David, that cometh in the name of the LORD: Hosanna in the highest"

- *Luke 19:37-38* – "The whole multitude of the disciples began to rejoice and praise God with a loud voice for all the mighty works that they had seen; Saying, Blessed (be) *the King* that cometh in the name of the LORD: peace in heaven, and glory in the highest"

- *John 12:13* – "And went forth to meet him, and cried, Hosanna: Blessed (is) *the King of Israel* that cometh in the name of the LORD"

Each writer has a different focus, stemming from the inspired structure of each Gospel. [5] The composite picture of Jesus seen in the four ways in which the people sang about Jesus is this: Jesus was the son of David who would sit on David's throne over God's kingdom of Israel. Rather than seeing different and conflicting words of praise, we should see the writers giving us an inspired summary of the people's words. It is probable that the people sang the words recorded in all the four records during Jesus' journey up to Jerusalem.

Over the previous three years, during Jesus' ministry, the opposition of the religious leaders to Jesus and his teaching had grown. Early in his ministry there was a recognition, voiced by Nicodemus on behalf of at least some Pharisees, that "we know that thou art a teacher come from God: [6] for no man can do these miracles that thou doest, except God be with him" (Jno. 3:2) This recognition of Jesus' origins changed over time: on one occasion they said, "We be not

---

5   It would be profitable, for example, to consider the way in which Matthew, more than any of the other Gospel writers, focuses on Jesus as "the son of David".

6   The phrase "from God", used by Nicodemus, forms a theme in John's Gospel: it is developed by Jesus' use of "from heaven" in his response to Nicodemus (Jno. 3:13), and passes into the rest of John's Gospel along with "from heaven".

born of fornication" (Jno. 8:41), whilst they said later, "We know that God spake unto Moses: as for this fellow, we know not from whence he is" (Jno. 9:29). It is not without interest, either, that "some of the Pharisees from among the multitude said unto him, Master, rebuke thy disciples" (Lk. 19:39).

It appears that the adulation accorded to Jesus continued during the next day also. This was despite the hiatus when he was approaching the city, and "wept over it", as Luke recounts (19:41). When Jesus was casting out the moneychangers, too, the people were still saying, "Hosanna to the son of David" (Mt. 21:15). On hearing this "the chief priest and scribes … were sore displeased".

In the name of the LORD

All four Gospels have the people praising Jesus as the one who would come "in the name of the LORD". So what were the people actually saying in using these words? A consideration of the phrase in the Old Testament will help to clarify what they understood by it. The phrase occurs 29 times in the Old Testament, but these four examples will serve to establish its meaning:

1. *Deuteronomy 18:22* – "When a prophet speaketh *in the name of the LORD*". This shows that when a prophet speaks words which he claims come from God he is not speaking his own words but is actually speaking on behalf of God. He is God's representative on earth.

2. *1 Samuel 17:45* – "Then said David … I come to thee *in the name of the LORD* of hosts". The passage demonstrates that David recognised he was not going against Goliath in his own strength, but that he was fighting God's battle, as Goliath had defied the armies

of Israel. David was God's representative in the battle, while Goliath was the Philistines' champion.

3. *2 Samuel 6:18* – "David ... blessed the people *in the name of the LORD* of hosts". When David brought the ark to Zion and dealt bread and wine to the people, he pronounced a blessing on them "in the name of the LORD". From this we learn that David did not see the work, nor the blessing, as his own. He saw himself as God's representative in placing the ark in the resting place which God had chosen.

4. *Psalm 118:26* – "Blessed be he that cometh *in the name of the LORD*". This passage from Psalm 118 speaks of one who would come in God's name – that is as His representative. This one who was to come was associated with salvation, as can be seen from the whole tenor of the Psalm.

We can conclude from these examples that the people viewed Jesus as God's representative as he journeyed towards Jerusalem. They clearly understood that he was not just an ordinary man. Instead, they saw him as one appointed by God to perform a specific task. But their expectations were ill-founded. This was not the time for the mighty king to come; it was the time for the suffering servant. Even so, they saw him as a special person, a man appointed by God to help them.

Weeping over the city

As Jerusalem came into view, Jesus wept over it and spoke of its destruction (Lk. 19:41-44). We have already seen that Jesus' weeping over the city was another echo of David's flight from Absalom. David "wept as he went up" (2 Sam.

15:30). David was weeping because he knew that he was going to be separated from the "city of the great king" (Ps. 48:2). Jesus wept as he saw the city because he knew that he was about to enter a city whose people would reject him, as was his father David when "Absalom stole the hearts of the men of Israel" (2 Sam. 15:6). So the joyous procession stopped as the city came into view.

Jesus probably dismounted from the animal on which he was riding in order to survey the city from the top of the hill across the Kidron Valley. Doubtless his demeanour puzzled the crowds, who were singing praises to him as he travelled towards the city. But their expectations did not match Jesus' own understanding of future events. He knew he was to die on the cross. He knew about the impending judgment of the city and its people at the hands of the Romans, and this was his prime concern at that time. David had fled from the city "lest (Absalom) smite the city with the edge of the sword" (2 Sam. 15:14). Jesus would shortly warn the disciples that Jerusalem's inhabitants would "fall by the edge of the sword, and shall be led away captive into all nations: and Jerusalem shall be trodden down of the Gentiles" (Lk. 21:24). [7] There are similarities between this lament over the city (in Luke 19) and the Olivet Prophecy (in Luke 21), and these are tabulated here:

Lament over Jerusalem		Olivet Prophecy		
Prophecy	Luke 19:42-44	Matthew	Mark	Luke
"compass thee"	19:43	24:20		

---

7   In the Olivet prophecy (in Luke 21) at the end of the third day before the Passover (*q.v.*).

Lament over Jerusalem		Olivet Prophecy		
Prophecy	Luke 19:42-44	Matthew	Mark	Luke
"children"	19:44	24:19	13:17	21:23
"not one stone"	19:44	24:2	13:2	

These similarities might lead to the superficial conclusion that the prophecy/lament in Luke 19 is the same event as the prophecy in Luke 21. But we have established that Luke 19 records events which took place *five* days before the Passover; and the chronology outlined at the beginning of this study shows that Luke 21 was spoken at the end of the *third* day before the Passover. Luke 19:42-44 was spoken early in the day on the way to Jerusalem, whereas Luke 21 was spoken at the end of the day, two days later. So we see that Jesus spoke of the destruction of the city at the beginning and at the end of the last week of his mortal life, even though the people were expecting exactly the opposite to happen.

As we shall see, the 'Olivet Prophecy' was given by Jesus towards the very end of his ministry; and it was directed specifically to his disciples and was designed to meet their particular needs. To this end, it contained a great deal of both warning and encouragement for them. By contrast, Jesus' prophecy/lament at the beginning of the last week was directed to a more general audience. John 12:12 records that "much people ... were come to the feast", and no doubt many of them would be travelling with Jesus and his disciples towards Jerusalem. They will have seen the tears of the Lord and heard his lament over the city. There is no warning in it, and no advice as to how to cope with the city's forthcoming destruction. It is simply a lament about the fact that the city would be destroyed because the people of the city failed to recognise the deliverance that was available through Jesus. That Jesus could speak like this at the beginning of this last week confirms that he knew that his message would finally be rejected, not only by the religious leaders but also by the people at large.

Jesus "looked round"

Mark informs us that when Jesus came to the temple, he "looked round about upon all things" (11:11). This simple action was highly significant. Jesus was treating the temple as a house which had been declared leprous. It was as if he had been given the task of examining it according to the Law of Leprosy.

Action	Law of Leprosy	Jesus
First look	Leviticus 14:34-38	John 2:13-14
Seven days later	Leviticus 14:39	Mark 11:11
If still leprous, remove stones	Leviticus 14:42	Mark 11:16
Destroy the house	Leviticus 14:44-45	Destruction of Jerusalem

The Law of Moses was quite specific in instructing Israel how they should deal with a 'leprous' house. If it was suspected that the house had leprosy, the priest was to be told and "Then the priest shall command that they empty the house, before the priest go into it to see the plague, that all that is in the house be not made unclean: and afterward the priest shall go in to see the house: And he shall look on the plague, and, behold, if the plague be in the walls of the house with hollow strakes, greenish or reddish, which in sight are lower than the wall; Then the priest shall go out of the house to the door of the house, and shut up the house seven days" (Lev. 14:36-38). After seven days the priest was to return and reassess the situation. If the house was still leprous, "Then the priest shall command that they take away the stones in which the plague is, and they shall cast them into an unclean place without the city: And he shall cause the house to be scraped within round about, and they shall pour out the dust that they scrape off without the city into an unclean place" (14:40-41). If this remedy did not work, "Then the priest shall come and look and, behold, if the plague be spread in the house, it is a fretting leprosy in the house: it is unclean. And he shall break down the house, the stones of it, and the timber thereof, and all the mortar of the house; and he shall carry them forth out of the city into an unclean place" (14:44-45).

There was thus a threefold inspection by the priest. On the first occasion the condition would be confirmed. The second visit examined the progress of the condition; and the third visit condemned the house if it was still plagued with the "fretting leprosy".

During the first Passover of his ministry Jesus cleansed the temple, as John 2:13-16 records:

> "And the Jews' Passover was at hand, and Jesus went up to Jerusalem, and found in the temple those that sold oxen and sheep and doves, and the changers of money sitting: and when he had made a scourge of small cords, he drove them all out of the temple, and the sheep, and the oxen; and poured out the changers' money, and overthrew the tables; and said unto them that sold doves, Take these things hence; make not my Father's house an house of merchandise."

This answers to the first visit of the priest under the Law of Leprosy. On that occasion "the priest shall command that they empty the house" (Lev. 14:36), which is exactly what Jesus did. This was the first indication that the city was being examined for leprosy.

On this fifth day before the Passover, three years later, Jesus "entered into Jerusalem, and into the temple: and when he had looked round about upon all things, and now the eventide was come, he went out unto Bethany" (Mk. 11:11) This visit answered to the second visit of the priest. On this occasion Jesus was assessing whether his first cleansing three years earlier had achieved the desired effect. His inspection confirmed that the house was still leprous. There was nothing left to do if things did not improve. Jesus knew that the house had to be destroyed.

He returned the next day and "went into the temple, and began to cast out them that sold and bought in the temple, and overthrew the tables of the moneychangers, and the seats of them that sold doves" (11:15). On this occasion we are told that Jesus "would not suffer that any man should carry any vessel through the temple" (11:16). This visit was the counterpart to the priest commanding "that they take away the stones in which the plague is, and ... cast them into an unclean place without the city" (Lev. 14:40).

These attempts at removing the leprosy were to no avail. When Jesus returned during the rest of the week he was rejected and abused and eventually crucified. So the city had to be destroyed. The destruction of the temple by the Romans in AD 70, when not one stone was left upon another, answers to the breaking down of the leprous house: "And he (the priest) shall break down the house, the stones of it, and the timber thereof, and all the morter of the house; and he shall carry them forth out of the city into an unclean place" (14:45).

Looking round about – Mark's Gospel

It would be reasonable to assume that Jesus often "looked round about" (Mk. 11:11) – that it was a common occurrence. But the phrase is, in fact, unique to Mark's Gospel. The occurrences apart from Mark 11:11 are as follows:

1. *Mark 3:5* – "And when he had looked round about on them with anger, being grieved for the hardness of their hearts, he saith unto the man, Stretch forth thine hand. And he stretched it out: and his hand was restored whole as the other".

2. *Mark 3:34* – "And he looked round about on them which sat about him, and said, Behold my mother and my brethren!"

3. *Mark 10:23* – "And Jesus looked round about, and saith unto his disciples, How hardly shall they that have riches enter into the kingdom of God!"

On each of these three occasions the context is similar: in some way or other, what is happening works against the purpose of God. On the first occasion a trap had been set: "And he entered again into the synagogue; and there was a man there which had a withered hand. And they watched him, whether he would heal him on the Sabbath day; that they might accuse him" (3:1-2). The religious leaders were trying to discredit Jesus. On the second occasion, by seeking to take Jesus away from his work, his mother and brothers were undermining his authority and work. On the third occasion, Jesus had called for commitment from the young ruler saying, "One thing thou lackest: go thy way, sell whatsoever thou hast, and give to the poor, and thou shalt have treasure in heaven: and come, take up the cross, and follow me" (10:21), but the man was not willing to make the sacrifice. He "went away grieved: for he had great possessions" (10:22). So this man, by not accepting the challenge, set a poor example to others, with the result that Jesus had to warn the people: "How hardly shall they that have riches enter into the kingdom of God!" (10:23).

On arriving at the temple, Jesus "looked round about" (11:11). He knew what was happening there – he had seen it all before. The use of the phrase "looked round about" highlights the fact that Jesus knew that the situation in the temple was running contrary to the ways of God. Like the priest condemning the leprous house, so Jesus was judging the condition of Israel as being in terminal decline.

Great expectations

It seems that the people had great expectations of Jesus as he entered Jerusalem. This was doubtless why they cried "Hosanna". Their expectation was that Jesus would overthrow the Roman occupation and establish the kingdom of God. Perhaps because he did nothing other than look round the temple started to sow seeds of doubt in the minds of those who would later cry, "Crucify him, crucify him" (Lk. 23:21). Whilst Luke (19:45) seems to indicate that Jesus cast out the money changers on this occasion, Mark (11:11-12) suggests that he simply left the city and went back to Bethany, and that the casting out of "them that sold and bought" (Mt. 21:12) took place on the next day.

The return to Bethany shows that Jesus and the disciples used Bethany as their base during the week (see Mark 11:12,19; 14:3). It might appear from Luke 21:37 ("And in the day time he was teaching in the temple; and at night he

went out, and abode in the mount that is called the Mount
of Olives"); but when we take account of the fact that
Bethany is on lower slopes of the Mount of Olives we can
see how the details in Mark 11:19 and 14:3 are reconciled
with what Luke says.

Matthew, Luke and the money changers

Matthew and Luke record the casting out of the money
changers as if it happened during this day, even though
the event actually took place the following day. There
must be a reason for the way in which Matthew records
these details. There are two things uniquely recorded by
Matthew which are attributed to this day. The first is the
fulfilment of Zechariah 9:9, which speaks of the coming
king and the cleansing of the temple.

Zechariah was speaking to the returning exiles. Nehemiah
had been supervising the building of the walls of Jerusalem,
but the priesthood was corrupt, whose condition was
addressed and criticised sometime later by the prophet
Malachi. [8] With the complicity of the religious leader of
Zechariah's day, Tobiah the Ammonite had polluted the
temple, so Nehemiah "cast forth all the household stuff of
Tobiah out of the chamber" (Neh. 13:8). Tobiah's ejection by
Nehemiah was the beginning of Nehemiah's cleansing of
the temple. There is a thematic link between this aspect of
Zechariah 9 and the entry of Jesus into Jerusalem. Zechariah
says on behalf of God, "Mine anger was kindled against
the shepherds" (Zech. 10:3) – a reflection of God's feelings
about those who should have been 'shepherding' Israel. So

---

8   Malachi 1:6 and 2:7 indicate that the priests were the primary
    recipients of Malachi's message.

Matthew, in addition to quoting the words of Zechariah 9:9, is also referring to the historical context of Nehemiah's cleansing of the temple.

That the casting out of the money changers is linked with the entry into Jerusalem on the previous day is reinforced by the way that Matthew continues with the thematic use of Psalm 118 by the people. He tells us that when Jesus was in the temple, there were those "saying Hosanna to the son of David" (Mt. 21:15), which is a variation on what the people cried as Jesus arrived at the city (21:9). On the first occasion the leaders had asked Jesus to stop his disciples singing Psalm 118; but Jesus had replied: "I tell you that, if these should hold their peace, the stones would immediately cry out" (Lk. 19:40). On this second occasion Jesus rebukes the same leaders with a quotation from Psalm 8:2, and asks them, "Have ye never read, Out of the mouth of babes and sucklings Thou hast perfected praise?" (Mt. 21:16). Comparing Psalm 8 and Jesus' use of it, and reflecting on what he did not quote is instructive:

Psalm 8	Matthew 21
v. 2: "Out of the mouth of babes and sucklings hast Thou *ordained strength because of thine enemies, that thou mightest still the enemy and the avenger*"	v. 16: "And said unto him, Hearest thou what these say? And Jesus saith unto them, Yea; have ye never read, Out of the mouth of babes and sucklings Thou hast *perfected praise?*"

So why does Jesus alter *"ordained strength"* to *"perfected praise"*? And why does he not say, *"because of thine enemies, that thou mightest still the enemy and the avenger"*?

We know that Psalm 8 speaks of the humanity of Jesus as the means whereby salvation has been obtained for us.

Hebrews 2:6-8 quotes Psalm 8:4-6, explaining that Jesus was "made a little lower than the angels for the suffering of death" (Heb. 2:9). A careful analysis of the language of Hebrews 2 makes the point about the humanity of Jesus even clearer:

- *v. 9* – For the suffering of death
- *v. 9* – taste death
- *v. 10* – perfect through sufferings
- *v. 14* – took part of the same (flesh)
- *v. 16* – seed of Abraham
- *v. 17* – like unto his brethren
- *v. 18* – suffered
- *v. 18* – tempted

Jesus knew that the aspirations of the people did not match reality. They expected a warrior king. He knew that he was going to die by the end of the week and that the same people who were praising him would call for his crucifixion. And yet, from the enthusiastic welcome of the people – their "perfected praise", as Matthew has it – Jesus will have received strength, as the Psalm records.

Jesus needed to be strengthened because those who were his adversaries as he entered the city and after he had cast out the money changers were the "enemies" spoken of in the Psalm. The Psalmist, by the Spirit, spoke of this, indicating to Jesus that he would receive this encouragement at this time. The leaders clearly knew Psalm 8; but they did not have the same understanding of it as Jesus. To them the Scriptures were a set of rules to govern the minutiae of life, whereas to Jesus they were his 'meat and drink'. They spoke to him in clear language, showing both how he should live and how his Father would care for him.

Summary of the fifth day before the Passover

The fifth day before the Passover began the work of the last week of Jesus' life. The triumphal entry into Jerusalem excited the people, who were expecting "that the kingdom of God should immediately appear" (Lk. 19:1). Yet Jesus wept over the city, knowing that it would be burnt to the ground by the Romans. On this occasion his lament was about the destruction of the city, in particular, whereas in the Olivet Prophecy (at the end of the third day before the Passover) his particular concern was that the disciples should be ready for the events he was speaking of. The people had great expectations of Jesus at this highly charged time of the Passover. The use of Zechariah 9:9 demonstrates that Jesus' mission was bigger than simply ridding Israel of the Romans. As the 'lowly' king 'having salvation', he was going to finish the work of redemption by giving himself as a sacrifice for sins. His disciples, and those caught up in the enthusiasm of his arrival at Jerusalem, understood none of these things. His inactivity in the temple, where he simply "looked round" (Mk. 11:11), must have caused the common people to wonder what was going to happen. The religious leaders would watch and discuss what Jesus was going to do. As Jesus left the city there was an air of great expectation – but neither the common people nor the religious leaders now knew what to expect.

Matthew speaks of the casting out of the money changers as if it happened on this day, even though it did not take place until the next day, because by the Spirit he was beginning to develop the link between the coming lowly king and the expectations of the people.

Finally, in Jesus' use of Psalm 8:2, we gain insight into Jesus' understanding of Scripture and how he saw it speaking to him and encouraging him.

Chapter 4:
Four days before the Passover

Events	Matthew	Mark	Luke	John	Time
Jesus curses the barren fig tree	21:18-19	11:11-18			AM
Cleansing of the temple	21:12-13[1]	11:15-18	19:45-48[1]		AM?
Some Greeks desire to see Jesus				12:20-36	
Jesus responds to unbelief of the crowd				12:37-50	
Return to Bethany		11:19			Late PM

The fourth day before the Passover is introduced by Jesus journeying into Jerusalem from Bethany once again. He had spent the previous night at Bethany, but we are given no information about what happened there. This is true of all the nights in this week except the last two nights of Jesus' life. But it is worth assuming that there would have been discussions

---

1 It is important to remember that, although Matthew and Luke's accounts of the cleansing of the temple are included here, the writers actually record the event *as if* it took place on the previous day.

between Jesus and his disciples, and perhaps also with Mary, Martha, Lazarus and Simon, about the events of the day. But the Spirit has chosen not to record any of those discussions.

On the way from Bethany

On the way to Jerusalem from Bethany – via the Mount of Olives – Jesus cursed a fig tree. But why? Why was he looking for fruit on it? Why was he hungry? Did Jesus have no breakfast that day?

That Jesus "hungered" may provide another insight into his humanity. He knew that within the week he would have been taken by cruel hands and crucified. He had told his disciples this on a number of occasions (for example, Matthew 17:22-23 and Mark 10:33). He was aware of what that entailed, just as most men and women in Israel would be aware of what was involved in crucifixion. But the Lord, with his understanding of the Old Testament prophets, would have an even clearer understanding of what was to take place. Having come so far in living a life which pleased his Father – a sinless life – Jesus also knew how much rested on him continuing his sinless life. Failure was a real possibility for him. This must have been so, otherwise the temptations of Jesus would have been a sham. He could have turned the stones into bread. He could have cast himself from the pinnacle of the temple. He could have used his outstanding skills to lead an uprising against the Romans and become the popular leader of Israel – and there must have been many more temptations. Yet greater trials and temptations were to come.

In times of stress the human appetite is diminished, and bodily functions are under reduced control. That Jesus was hungry, despite having only recently left Bethany, is perhaps an indication of the stress he was enduring. Maybe he had risen early to pray and, having spent so much time in prayer, he had left Bethany without breakfast. Although we do not know this for sure, we do well to reflect on the possible effects on the Lord's human frame of his foreknowledge of the impending events.

Cursing the fig tree

The first thing to notice about Matthew 21 is that the chapter's details cover three days.[2] Through the Spirit, each Gospel writer was developing independent themes and links distinct from the chronological nature of the record. The event described in Matthew 21:19 (*"And when he saw a fig tree in the way, (Jesus) said unto it, Let no fruit grow on thee henceforward forever. And presently the fig tree withered away"*) took place in the morning of the fourth day before the Passover. The conversation recorded in verses 19-22 (*"And when the disciples saw it, they marveled, saying, How soon is the fig tree withered away! Jesus answered and said unto them, Verily I say unto you, If ye have faith, and doubt not, ye shall not only do this which is done to the fig tree, but also if ye shall say unto this mountain, Be thou removed, and be thou cast into the sea; it shall be done. And all things, whatsoever ye shall ask in prayer, believing, ye shall receive"*) took place the next morning as the disciples and Jesus were travelling back to Jerusalem. We know this is so because in the parallel account in Mark (11:12-13) we read: "And on the morrow, when they were come from Bethany, he was hungry. And seeing a fig tree afar off". We must, therefore, conclude

---

2 Verses 1-17 cover the first day; verses 18-19 cover the second day; and the third day begins in verse 20.

that the response of the disciples which Matthew records is part of the lesson to be learned from this event. Jesus cursed the fig tree on the morning of the fourth day before the Passover, and the disciples saw that it was withered on the morning of the third day before the Passover.

Why curse the fig tree?

So why did Jesus curse the fig tree? We know that he "hungered" (Mt. 21:16); but being hungry does not provide a sufficient reason to curse a fig tree. The record tells us that it was not the time when fruit would be expected, "for the time of figs was not yet" (Mk. 11:13), and Jesus will have known that. So his response at finding no figs on the tree was not simply a fit of pique on finding nothing for him to eat.

The conclusion must be that Jesus intended to teach his disciples an object lesson: the cursing of the fig tree would provide the vehicle through which the lesson would be taught. But what was the lesson, and which Old Testament Scriptures was the event based on?

The lesson of the fig tree

The prophet Hosea reveals that God looked upon the fathers of the Jewish nation as "the firstripe in the fig tree at her first time" (Hosea 9:10); so it is reasonable to conclude that the fig tree represents Israel. But why was Jesus looking for fruit when it was not the season for it? The lesson relies on the way in which Israel are presented as a fig in Hosea. Whilst a natural tree bears fruit at a specific time in the year, Israel should have borne fruit all the time. But Hosea describes Israel as a fig tree only bearing fruit at a specific time in its annual life cycle.

Israel were not bearing fruit during the lifetime of Jesus. As he entered Jerusalem five days before the Passover, the common people (but not the religious leaders) had hailed him as their blessed king. But they did not realise that Jesus had come to "save his people from their sins" (Mt. 1:21). Nor did the leaders recognise Jesus as the person he really was – "the Lamb of God". They thought he was "born of fornication" (Jno. 8:41). The fickle enthusiasm of the common people and the meticulous religious lives of the religious leaders were not the kind of fruit that God was expecting from them. The common people misunderstood the Scriptures, and the religious leaders were "going about to establish their own righteousness" (Rom. 10:3).

The disciples' amazement

Whereas Mark presents the cursing of the fig tree and the disciples seeing the withered fig tree on two separate days, Matthew's record would lead us to conclude that both events took place on the same day. Indeed, if we only read Matthew we would conclude that the fig tree withered before their eyes – as they watched. But consider Matthew's words again:

> "And when he saw a fig tree in the way, he came to it, and found nothing thereon, but leaves only, and said unto it, Let no fruit grow on thee henceforward forever. And presently the fig tree withered away. And when the disciples saw (it), they marvelled, saying, How soon is the fig tree withered away!" (Mt. 21:19-20).

In recording the events in this way and dislocating the time frame, Matthew is seeking to highlight the *effect* of the event on the disciples. Whilst Mark says it was "Peter" (Mk. 11:21) who drew Jesus' attention to the withered fig tree, Matthew (21:20) tells us that it was the "disciples" who drew the Lord's attention to the tree. Matthew's record of Jesus' response is short and to the point. He tells us that Jesus emphasised the need to believe that prayers will be answered. This is said against the background of the comments that faith will move a mountain.

Mark, as well as advising us that the withering of the fig tree was noticed on the morning of the next day, presents a more detailed account of Jesus' lesson. He introduces the concept of forgiveness, saying: "And when ye stand praying, forgive, if ye have ought against any: that your Father also which is in heaven may forgive you your trespasses. But if ye do not forgive, neither will your Father which is in heaven forgive your trespasses" (Mk. 11:25-26).

We have already seen similar teaching twice in the Gospel records. In the Sermon on the Mount, Jesus told his disciples: "And forgive us our debts, as we forgive our debtors ... For if ye forgive men their trespasses, your heavenly Father will also forgive you: But if ye forgive not men their trespasses, neither will your Father forgive your trespasses" (Mt. 6:12-15). At a later date, too, in answer to the request "teach us to pray" (Lk. 11:1), Jesus used almost identical words. So it seems that Mark is presenting this aspect of Jesus' teaching for the first time in his account, although this is the third time that Jesus has made this point. At this point in his ministry, therefore, Jesus is once again teaching his disciples the importance of the right attitude towards the failings of others.

Fig trees in the last week

It may be inferred that the fig tree which Jesus cursed was on the Mount of Olives. As Jesus and the disciples moved towards Jerusalem from Bethany, he would have crossed the lower reaches of the Mount of Olives on his way into the city.

The disciples saw the withered fig tree on the morning of the third day before the Passover. In the late afternoon of that day Jesus spoke to his disciples on the Mount of Olives, as Matthew records (24:3). This was the occasion of what we call 'The Olivet Prophecy', in which Jesus used the fig tree as the basis of a central point of the prophecy: "Behold the fig tree", he said (Lk. 21:29), perhaps even pointing to the tree he had cursed the previous day. So the lesson of the fig tree which Jesus cursed on the morning of the fourth day before the Passover finishes with the Olivet prophecy. [3]

The cleansing of the temple

Matthew had a particular reason to associate the cleansing of the temple with the 'triumphal' entry into Jerusalem (which happened the day before). We will consider the event, with Mark, in its chronological sequence. In so doing, we will see other issues being brought to our notice by the Gospel writers.

This was the second time that Jesus cleansed the temple. John 2:13-17 records the first occasion, which took place three years earlier, during the first Passover feast of Jesus' ministry. Selling animals for sacrifice was permitted under the Law of Moses:

> "And if the way be too long for thee, so that thou art not able to carry it; or if the place be too far from thee, which

---

3   That Jesus was using the fig tree as a lesson is reinforced by the other records, which say: "Now learn a parable of the fig tree" (Mt. 24:32; Mk. 13:28).

the LORD thy God shall choose to set His name there,
when the LORD thy God hath blessed thee: Then shalt
thou turn it into money, and bind up the money in thine
hand, and shalt go unto the place which the LORD thy
God shall choose: And thou shalt bestow that money
for whatsoever thy soul lusteth after, for oxen, or for
sheep, or for wine, or for strong drink, or for whatsoever
thy soul desireth: and thou shalt eat there before the
LORD thy God, and thou shalt rejoice, thou, and thine
household" (Deut. 14:24-26).

So the selling of animals was not, of itself, the problem.
Jesus was not objecting to the fact that men and women
were buying animals for sacrifice. Instead, he was objecting
to the way in which it was being done.

Consider for a moment the magnitude of Jesus' actions.
The twelve disciples were with Jesus on the temple mount;
but none of the Gospels suggests that they were involved
with Jesus in cleansing the temple: he acted entirely alone.
Herod's temple mount area occupied around 20 acres,
a large part of which was given over to the temple. It is
probable that Jesus cast out the money changers at the
south end of the temple, in the market area. His behaviour
will certainly have aroused concern. The religious leaders
must have been extremely disturbed at his actions. The
riot of running animals and overturned tables would meet
with their strong disapproval – and not least because these
men gained a handsome income from these activities.
They controlled the market and received a percentage
of the business transacted. Passover time was also a time
of tension in Jerusalem for the occupying Roman army.
There was a fortress at the north-western corner of the

temple mount, from which the Roman garrison would be able to observe events on the temple mount. On seeing the animals scurrying away and hearing the commotion, they were doubtless greatly concerned to stop what they may have thought was a riot. Jesus' behaviour will have been carefully calculated to obtain the desired outcome: he wanted to demonstrate the extortion being practised by the money changers and those who sold animals. But he did not seek to be arrested by the Romans for causing a riot, nor to fall into the hands of the religious leaders at that time.

Nehemiah and Tobiah

On his second visit to Jerusalem, Nehemiah found that the spiritual state of the priesthood was corrupt. The whole of the prophecy of Malachi addresses this problem. One particular feature of the corruption was manifest in the way that an Ammonite was housed within the temple. Eliashib, the high priest, prepared "a chamber in the courts of the house of God" for Tobiah (Neh. 13:7). On seeing this, Nehemiah "cast forth all the household stuff of Tobiah out of the chamber" (13:8). So the corruption of the temple worship by the priests and other leaders in the time of Jesus was not a new thing. The casting out of the money changers is another example of a faithful man responding to the depravity of the priesthood.

The two quotations

As he cast out the money changers, Jesus said: "It is written, *My house shall be called the house of prayer* (Isa. 56:7); but ye have made it *a den of thieves* (Jer. 7:11)" (Mt. 21:13). In saying this, Jesus was drawing together two passages from the Old Testament, in order to highlight two aspects of the circumstances of his day which were both wrong and which served to explain the desperate state of the nation at this time. Whereas the common people were looking for a warrior king to save them from the Romans, the bigger need was for the nation to be saved from its sinfulness.

Isaiah 56:1 taught that God's 'salvation was near'; and therefore the man "that keepeth the Sabbath from polluting it, and keepeth his hand from doing any evil" would be 'blessed' (56:2). The salvation that was 'near' was Jesus. The Sabbath that was being polluted was the Sabbath of the Passover. It was being polluted with the buying and selling of animals for gain. The Jews were about to reject the salvation that their God was offering in Jesus while they went through the ritual of the Passover. Because of this rejection, salvation was to be offered to the Gentiles. Isaiah 56:4-7 spoke eloquently of this:

> "For thus saith the LORD unto the eunuchs that keep My Sabbaths ... even unto them will I give in Mine house and within My walls a place and a name better than of sons and of daughters: I will give them an everlasting name that shall not be cut off. Also the sons of the stranger, that join themselves to the LORD, to serve Him, and to love the name of the LORD to be His servants, every one that keepeth the Sabbath from polluting it, and taketh hold of My covenant; even them will I bring to My holy mountain, and make them joyful in My house of prayer: their burnt offerings and their sacrifices shall be accepted upon Mine altar; for Mine house shall be called an house of prayer for all nations."

We have already commented on the similarity between Nehemiah and Jesus removing items from the temple.

Reviewing Zechariah 5 at this point is interesting in this connection also. Zechariah had prophesied shortly before the second visit of Nehemiah to Jerusalem, and so his message would have been known by the Jews at the time of Nehemiah's visit.

Zechariah wrote of "wickedness" (5:8). In that context he speaks of a "flying roll" (5:2), whose dimensions match the size of the porch before Solomon's temple (1 Kgs. 6:3). He speaks of thieves being "cut off" (5:3), just as Jeremiah spoke of the house of God as "a den of thieves" (Jer. 7:11) Then Zechariah speaks of destruction by using words from the Law of Leprosy as meted out to a leprous house, as shown in the following table:

Leviticus 14	Zechariah 5
v. 45 – "carry them forth"	*v.* 4 – "bring it forth"
v. 45 – "stones"/ "timber"	*v.* 4 – "timber"/ "stones"

Jesus fulfils the prophecy in Zechariah 5 and speaks of the fulfilment of Isaiah 56 and Jeremiah 7 in reproving the Jewish leaders for their greed and exclusivity. The way in which Zechariah 5 likens what he saw to the leprous house further links Jesus' entry into Jerusalem and the cleansing of the temple.

The middle wall of partition

Isaiah had spoken of the house serving as "a house of prayer *for all nations*", but Herod's temple was used exclusively for Jewish worship. The Jews, in the way that they had set out the courts in the temple, prevented Gentiles from approaching near to the inner sanctuary. Surrounding the temple area was a wall – the "middle wall of partition" – which a Gentile was not permitted to pass (Eph. 2:14). [4] In fact, at the gates in the wall where Jews could pass through, there were signs stating that any Gentile who passed beyond this point would be responsible for his own death. Thus segregation between Jew and Gentile was established, and the house of God was not a house of prayer for all nations.

By joining the quotation from Isaiah 56 with Jeremiah 7:11 ("but ye have made it a den of thieves"), Jesus was drawing the attention of the Jews to the consequences of polluting the temple – Jeremiah prophesied immediately prior to the destruction of the temple by the Babylonians.

Jeremiah had been told to "stand in the gate of the LORD's house, and proclaim there this word, and say, Hear the word of the LORD, all ye of Judah, that enter in at these gates to worship the LORD. Thus saith the LORD of hosts, the God of Israel, Amend your ways and your doings, and I will cause you to dwell in this place" (7:2-3). But the people did not listen to Jeremiah's words and so the temple was destroyed by the Babylonians.

Jesus had already told the people on the previous day:

> "If thou (Jerusalem) hadst known, even thou, at least in this thy day, the things which belong unto thy peace! But now they are hid from thine eyes. For the days shall

---

4　In Ephesians Paul, in speaking of the removal of the "middle wall of partition", writes of the removal of the Jew/Gentile distinction for those "in Christ". The accusation of the Jews, that Paul had taken Trophimus into the temple (Acts 21:29), is the background to the Ephesians' experience.

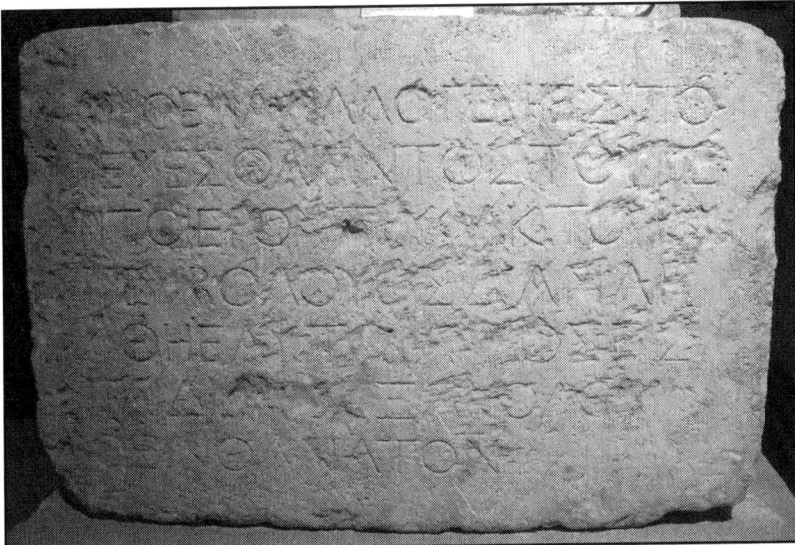

"No intruder is allowed in the courtyard and within the wall surrounding the temple. Whoever enters will invite death for himself!"

Image: © Jona Lendering / Licence: CC0 1.0 Universal. Museum: Istanbul, Arkeoloji Müzesi.

come upon thee, that thine enemies shall cast a trench about thee, and compass thee round, and keep thee in on every side, and shall lay thee even with the ground, and thy children within thee; and they shall not leave in thee one stone upon another; because thou knewest not the time of thy visitation" (Lk. 19:42-44).

In the context of his entry into Jerusalem, amidst the acclaim of his disciples and the people, Jesus had foretold the overthrow of the nation of Israel and of Jerusalem in particular. In casting out the money changers and teaching the people, Jesus was explaining how they had not recognised the time of their "visitation" (19:42). The LORD had "visited His people" (1:68), but they were so busy with their own pursuits that they did not recognise Him.

Missing the point

Because the chief priests and other religious leaders hated Jesus and loved their positions of self-importance they did not recognise that he was doing a good work. As a direct consequence of his teaching, "the scribes and chief priests … sought how they might destroy him: for they feared him" (Mk. 11:18).

We would see Jesus

By contrast with the leaders' unbelief and hatred of Jesus, "there were certain Greeks among them that came up to worship … saying, Sir, we would see Jesus" (Jno. 12:20-21). Although John does not say precisely when these "Greeks" came looking for the Lord, it is reasonable to conclude that this happened immediately after Jesus had cleansed the temple and asserted that it was a "house of prayer" (Mt. 21:13), quoting Isaiah 56:7.

These Greeks had come "to worship at the feast" (Jno. 12:20). It is probable that these "Greeks" were Hellenistic Greek Jews, though they may actually have been Gentiles. The original word for "Greeks" here is translated "Greeks" or "Grecians" 20 times and "Gentiles" 7 times in the Authorised Version. A typical example where it clearly refers to Greek Jews is in Acts 6:1: "And in those days, when the number of the disciples was multiplied, there arose a murmuring of the Grecians (Gk., **hellane**) against the Hebrews, because their widows were neglected in the daily ministration". Since the gospel message had not yet been taken directly to the Gentiles and the events recorded were in Jerusalem, these widows had to be Greek Jews.

But as time passed and the gospel was taken to the Gentiles, the meaning of the word *hellane* was extended to include non-Jews – true Gentiles – as can be seen from Romans 2:9-10:

> "Tribulation and anguish, upon every soul of man that doeth evil, of the Jew first, and also of the Gentile (*hellane*); but glory, honour, and peace, to every man that worketh good, to the Jew first, and also to the Gentile (*hellane*)".

This passage clearly makes the point that by the time that Paul was writing the gospel had been extended to non-Jews, and not just the Greek-speaking Jews. A more detailed review of the use of *hellane*, which is outside the scope of this study, shows that in the time of Jesus the word referred to Hellenistic Jews – that is Jews who were not born in the land of Israel. Only later was the more general meaning 'Gentile' (*i.e.*, non-Jew) given to the word.

The problem described in Acts 6:1 ("And in those days, when the number of the disciples was multiplied, there arose a murmuring of the Grecians against the Hebrews, because their widows were neglected in the daily ministration") demonstrates that there was tension between the Hebrews – that is, Jews born in the land of Israel – and Greek-speaking Jews (who were viewed as inferior Jews by their Hebrew brethren). The Jews saw different degrees of "Jewishness" amongst Jews: Paul, for example, imitates the pride and exclusivity of those who "are of the flesh" when he writes that he was "circumcised the eighth day, of the stock of

Israel, of the tribe of Benjamin, an *Hebrew of the Hebrews*; as touching the law, a Pharisee" (Phil. 3:5).

Emboldened by Jesus' words

The Greeks, who had come to worship at the feast, though Jews, would feel their isolation in the environment of worship in Jerusalem. The self-righteousness of the Pharisees, and the way in which the Hellenistic Jews were denigrated, would have made them feel somewhat isolated from their Jewish brethren and their law, even though they had come to keep the Passover in line with the requirement of the Law of Moses: "Three times in a year shall all thy males appear before the LORD thy God in the place which He shall choose; in the feast of unleavened bread" (Deut. 16:16). Arriving at the feast, these Greeks doubtless heard Jesus' preaching, and maybe even saw him casting out the money changers on the temple mount. Emboldened by his words about the temple being a "house of prayer" for people of all nationalities (Mt. 21:13; Mk. 11:17; Lk. 19:46), these people sought Jesus out.

Their initial approach was to Philip (Jno. 12:21). This is in keeping with others who, out of respect for Jesus, did not seek immediately to trouble him with their request. A centurion sent his servant to seek for Jesus' assistance. When Jesus approached, the message was sent by friends: "And when he (Jesus) was now not far from the house, the centurion sent friends to him, saying unto him, Lord, trouble not thyself: for I am not worthy that thou shouldest enter under my roof" (Lk. 7:6).

Such an event would have been a great comfort to the Lord at this time. While the Jews were polluting the temple and going about to kill Jesus, there were Greeks who wished to be associated with him and the temple. This is one of a number of events during this last week when things happened which would have given Jesus some comfort. As such, they are an illustration of how God used circumstances, providentially, to encourage His son.

This contrast between the scribes and chief priests on the one hand and the Greeks on the other is the reason why John tells us: "But though he had done so many miracles before them, yet they believed not on him" (Jno. 12:37). The Jews were fulfilling the words of Isaiah when he wrote: "Who hath believed our report, and to whom is the arm of the LORD revealed?" (Isa. 53:1) – a passage which is also quoted in John 12:38. The "arm of the LORD" had been revealed to the Gentiles.

This Jewish unbelief had also been predicted in Isaiah 6:9-10; but all was not yet lost, for we learn that "among the chief rulers also many believed on him; but because of the Pharisees they did not confess him, lest they should be put out of the synagogue" (Jno. 12:42). Two such "chief rulers" would ultimately come out into the open and admit their belief in Jesus: both Nicodemus and Joseph of Arimathea are included among those spoken of here by John.

Summary of the fourth day before the Passover

Jesus spent the night in Bethany. On his way into Jerusalem from there with the disciples he cursed the fig tree because he was hungry. It is suggested that the hunger demonstrated that he was under pressure at the prospect of the events of the upcoming day.

On entering the temple he cleansed it of money changers. This was the second time that he had done this during his ministry. The first time was during the first Passover of his ministry, three years earlier.

The day ended with Jesus returning to Bethany once again.

Chapter 5:
Three days before the Passover

The 'longest' day

It is noticeable that a large proportion of each Gospel record is devoted to this last week in Jesus' life. We have now arrived at the third day before the Passover. This is, in Scripture, the longest day in the life of Jesus. Of course, all days were the same length in terms of linear time; but the Spirit has chosen to record more about this day than any other day in the life of Jesus. In Matthew, the events of this day cover almost five chapters. The day begins in Matthew 21:18 and ends in Matthew 25:46.

On the way into Jerusalem in the morning

Events	Matthew	Mark	Luke	John	Time
Disciples see the withered fig tree	21:18-22	11:20-26			AM
Priests question Jesus' authority	21:23-27	11:27-33	20:1-8		
Which son did his father's will?	21:28-32				
Parable of the vineyard	21:33-46	12:1-12	20:9-19		

Events	Matthew	Mark	Luke	John	Time
Parable of the wedding banquet	22:1-14				

The records of this particular day have two distinguishing features: first, they contain an account of the most prolonged and powerful onslaught of the Jewish authorities against Jesus; and secondly, they mark the end of Jesus' public ministry. From late in the afternoon of this day, Jesus will never be seen teaching publicly again. His focus turns from the religious leaders and the common people to the twelve disciples: his closest followers become the primary focus of his attention and of his words.

The priests' question, "by what authority doest thou these things?" (Mt. 21:23) is a response to Jesus' actions on the previous day. On entering the temple he had "cast out all them that sold and bought in the temple, and overthrew the tables of the moneychangers, and the seats of them that sold doves" (Mt. 21:12). In doing this, Jesus was attacking the very lifestyle of the priests, who were accustomed to gaining a lucrative income from the practice.

By asking the priests, in his reply, to reflect on the authority of John the Baptist, Jesus is not trying to avoid the issue they have raised. John had already testified that Jesus was "the lamb of God" (Jno. 1:29), and we know that many of the leaders went out into the wilderness to hear John (Mt. 3:7). We also know that "the Pharisees and lawyers rejected the counsel of God against themselves, being not baptised of him" (Lk. 7:30). Because they were unwilling to accept

John's testimony about Jesus, it followed quite naturally that they would not accept anything Jesus said about himself. So Jesus was not avoiding the issue of authority; instead he was focusing the leaders' minds on an unresolved issue. When they were able to form a judgment about John's baptism then they would be in a position to evaluate Jesus' authority. But they were unwilling to say what they thought about the source of John's authority because they "feared the people" (Mk. 11:32). Unable to reject the teaching of John openly, therefore, they responded feebly, "We cannot tell" (11:33).

Fear and hypocrisy

There were a number of occasions – of which this was the first during the last week of Jesus' life – when the leaders "feared the people". The second was after he had told the parable of the wicked husbandmen (Mt. 21:33-45; Mk. 12:1-12; Lk. 20:9-19). The third was the next day, when they were consulting how they might take Jesus (Lk. 22:2).

The phrase 'feared the people' catches the mental state of Saul when he failed to kill the Amalekites (1 Sam. 15:24). Saul's excuse for not carrying out the will of God was because of his fear of the people. So now, in not doing God's will because they feared the people, the Jewish religious leaders showed the same attitude as Saul. They, like Saul, were more interested in the praise of men than in the approval of God. This was their downfall.

Jesus could have left them at this point and continued with his tasks for the day. If we had been in his shoes, we might well have turned away from them with the smug self-satisfaction of knowing that we had silenced our critics. But the Lord was not like that. He was concerned that these men should be made to face up to their hypocrisy; and that was why he told them three relevant parables:

Parable	Matthew	Mark	Luke
1. Which son did his father's will?	21:28-32		
2. The parable of the vineyard	21:33-46	12:1-12	20:9-19
3. The parable of the wedding garment	22:1-14		

All three parables were directed at the attitude of the religious leaders.

Earlier that same day, in response to Jesus' question about the baptism of John, the leaders had to say that they could not tell where John's authority to baptise had come from. They were unwilling to commit themselves on the matter; so they, in effect, remained silent. The three parables which Jesus now tells are designed to force the leaders to speak.

Which son did his father's will?

The first parable considers two sons and their responses. The first son refuses to do as his father asks him, but afterwards repents and goes, whereas the second son says he will go but fails to do so (Mt. 21:29-30). Jesus then asks the religious leaders: "Whether of them twain did the will of his father?" The leaders are obliged to answer, and so, "They say unto him, The first" (Mt. 21:31). This parable relates to the issue of his authority and John's. This is clear from the way in which Jesus continued by saying: "Verily I say unto you, that the publicans and the harlots go into the kingdom of God before you. For John came unto you in the way of righteousness, and ye believed him not: but the publicans and the harlots believed him: and ye, when ye had seen it, repented not afterward, that ye might believe him" (Mt. 21:31-32). Like John's authority, the Lord's came from God; but the leaders would not accept the authority of either, even though they had been given sufficient evidence to recognise the divine authority of both.

The parable of the vineyard and its Old Testament echoes

The second parable, the parable of the vineyard, by carefully using language from Isaiah 5 and Psalm 80, presents a picture of a householder's response to the various ways in which his servants have been treated. The final act of sending "his son" (Mt. 21:37) answers to the sending of Jesus. The murder of the son in the parable, because he was "the heir" (Mt. 21:38), would happen in 'real life' by the end of the week!

The elements of the parable are: a planted vineyard, a hedge, a winepress and a tower. The vineyard was let out to husbandmen while the owner went into a far country. His servants were sent for the fruit, but they were beaten, killed and stoned. Further servants were sent, and they were treated similarly. Finally, the owner's son was sent, but he was killed. The question "what will the Lord of the vineyard do" was asked, to which the answer was given: "He will destroy ...". Many of these elements of the parable are drawn from the Old Testament:

Parable element	Psalm	Isaiah	Jeremiah
Planted vineyard	80:8	5:1	2:21
Hedge	80:12		
Winepress		5:2	

Parable element	Psalm	Isaiah	Jeremiah
Tower		5:2	
Let out to husbandmen			
Servant stoned	[2 Chron. 24:21]		
"He will destroy"		5:6	

A vine supposed to bring forth fruit

The figure of the vine passed into Jesus' teaching during the remainder of the week before the crucifixion; and the figure had deep roots in the Jewish Scriptures.

The Old Testament clearly indicates that the house of Israel was a 'vine' which had been "brought out of Egypt" (Hos. 11:1) and "planted" (Isa. 5:2) in the land which had been prepared for it. As such, the nation was expected to bring forth fruit to God under the care of the priests and religious leaders. But Israel's history demonstrates that the Jewish people rarely brought forth fruit, despite God "rising early" and sending the prophets (Jer. 11:7). In the days of Hezekiah the prophet Isaiah spoke the parable of the vineyard, recorded in Isaiah 5. Micah, a contemporary of Isaiah, taking up the message, prophesied that Jerusalem would be "plowed as a field" (Mic. 3:12) – intended as a judgement from God in Hezekiah's day. But Hezekiah repented and humbled himself before God (2 Chr. 32:26), and the "vineyard" was not destroyed at that time. At a later date, as a means of saving the life of the prophet Jeremiah in the days of King Jehoiakim, the elders of Judah were able to refer back to Hezekiah's repentance in these terms:

> "Micah the Morasthite prophesied in the days of Hezekiah king of Judah, and spake to all the people

of Judah, saying, Thus saith the LORD of hosts; Zion shall be plowed like a field, and Jerusalem shall become heaps, and the mountain of the house as the high places of a forest. Did Hezekiah king of Judah and all Judah put him at all to death? Did he not fear the LORD, and besought the LORD, and the LORD repented Him of the evil which He had pronounced against them? Thus might we procure great evil against our souls" (Jer. 26:18-19).

The leaders to whom Jesus was speaking would be familiar with the biblical background to his parable of the vineyard and its implications. If only they had been willing to listen to 'the son', the message could have been very powerful to save them from destruction.

What will the Lord of the vineyard do?

In order to force the leaders to confront their mental state, Jesus asked the question, "When the lord therefore of the vineyard cometh, what will he do unto those husbandmen?" (Mt. 21:40). But before the leaders were able to answer the question, the answer was given by the common people. They said: "He will miserably destroy those wicked men, and will let out his vineyard unto other husbandmen, which shall render him the fruits in their seasons" (Mt. 21:41). Jesus endorsed this response, as Mark 12:9 and Luke 20:16 indicate. The response of the leaders was, "God forbid"; and in saying this, they "perceived that (Jesus) spake of them" (Mt. 21:45). They did not heed the words of the parable, or reflect on the common people's answer, nor even their own horror at the predicted outcome.[1]

---

1 Jerusalem was overthrown by the Romans some forty years later.

At this point in the discussion Jesus draws the attention of the religious leaders to Psalm 118:22, by asking them, "Did ye never read in the Scriptures, the stone which the builders rejected, the same is become the head of the corner: this is the LORD's doing, and it is marvellous in our eyes?" (Mt. 21:42). The Lord's question about Psalm 118 is very significant at this point.

Two days earlier the people had been singing parts of Psalm 118 as Jesus made his way to Jerusalem on the animals. The people also used some of the same words the next day when Jesus cast out the money changers. Despite not wanting to hear the words of Psalm 118 being sung to Jesus, those same leaders, having heard the parable of the vineyard, were now forced to reflect on the words of the psalm again. Jesus continues, saying, "The kingdom of God shall be taken from you" (Mt. 21:43); and he thereby reinforces what the people had been saying, and identifies himself as the "stone which the builders rejected". What follows is an appeal from Jesus to those leaders to repent and to recognise their Messiah – his appeal for repentance is couched in the words of Isaiah 8: "… whosoever shall fall on this stone shall be broken" (21:44).

The context of Isaiah 8 is about the coming of Emmanuel (v. 8) to deliver Israel. In the days of Hezekiah, God was promising deliverance; but some were seeking for help from other sources. Isaiah said that such help would be futile (v. 10). Rather than seeking help elsewhere, the people were called on to "sanctify the LORD of hosts" (v. 13), who would be a "stone of stumbling" to those who would not acknowledge Him. Those who rejected Him would "fall and be broken" (v. 15). The appeal was clear and uncomplicated: they were being called on to recognise

Emmanuel as their divinely appointed saviour. But sadly, they were so intent on establishing their own status that they were ultimately rejected. As Jesus expressed it, they were to be ground to powder (Mt. 21:44). They were to suffer the fate of the kingdoms of this world that were to be destroyed and replaced by the stone cut out of the mountain without hands (Dan. 2:32-35).

Isaiah 5 predicted the removal of the hedge and the treading down of the vineyard – the house of Israel. Later on during the same day, Jesus spoke to the disciples on the Mount of Olives. In response to their question as to when "these things" (the destruction of Jerusalem) would happen (Lk. 21:7), Jesus replies, "Jerusalem *shall be trodden down* of the Gentiles" (21:24), quoting Isaiah 5 again ("I will tell you what I will do to my vineyard … It *shall be trodden down*" (Isa. 5:5). This 'Olivet Prophecy' was given as a private explanation of some of the details of the parable of the vineyard. The destruction of Jerusalem, which was accomplished by the Romans in AD 70, was a fulfilment of the parable, which in turn was an exposition of Isaiah 5. The absence of a repentant heart made the destruction a certainty, unlike in the days of Hezekiah. Hezekiah, on being presented with the predicted judgement, repented. The leaders in Jesus' day did not.

An old warning ignored

Nor was Jesus' parable of the vineyard in Matthew 21 the first time this warning had been given to these leaders. John the Baptist had already given a similar warning which had gone unheeded. Three and a half years earlier, when John was baptising at Aenon, the Pharisees came to investigate. And when John saw them, he cried out: "O generation of vipers, who hath warned you to flee from the wrath to come? Bring forth therefore fruits meet for repentance ... the axe is laid unto the root of the trees: therefore every tree which bringeth not forth good fruit is hewn down, and cast into the fire" (Mt. 3:7-10). Yet just as they had rejected the counsel of John the Baptist, so these same leaders rejected Jesus, and "sought to lay hands on him" (21:36). The only thing which prevented them from taking any action was that "they feared the multitude, because they (the multitude) took him for a prophet" (21:46).

Responding to the Lord: a question for us

Turning the spotlight on ourselves at this point, we may well ask, 'Is our motivation driven by a desire to please the Father, or are we menpleasers, compromised by what we think that others will think of us?' How would we answer the Lord's question, "What will the lord of the vineyard do?". Would we remain silent because we are convicted by the Lord? Would we join with the common people and see the obvious outcome of such rebellion? Or would we join with the Pharisees, saying "God forbid", because we want to continue in our own way, with scant regard to the call of the Master to bring forth fruit?

The marriage of the king's son

The third parable that Jesus gives here is about the marriage of the king's son. The wedding was furnished with guests who were "both bad and good" (Mt. 22:10), because those who had been invited at first declined the invitation. But there was one of the guests "which had not on a wedding garment" (22:11). Just like the religious leaders, when this man was confronted about his cavalier attitude to the requirements of the king he was "speechless" (22:12). Like this man in the parable, the scribes and Pharisees offered no answer to Jesus when he asked them about the baptism of John.

What these leaders did do, however, revealed yet again that the Word of God had no effect on their consciences. "Then went the Pharisees, and took counsel how they might entangle (Jesus) in his talk" (22:15). And this led directly to three attacks on Jesus by a coalition of the most unlikely alliances.

These three attacks were triggered by the leaders' desire to "take hold of (Jesus') words, that so they might deliver him unto the power and authority of the governor" (Lk. 20:20). This statement shows, first, that even this close to the death of Jesus the religious leaders still had not formulated a plan to arrest him. And this was no doubt why, when Judas approached the leaders only two days before the Passover (Mt. 26:2), they were so eager to pay him for his help when he asked them, "What will ye give me, and I will deliver him unto you?" (26:15).

The first attack on Jesus: taxes

Events	Matthew	Mark	Luke	John	Time
Paying taxes to Caesar	22:15-22	12:13-17	20:20-26		

Operating, perhaps, on the principle of 'safety in numbers', the Pharisees "sent out unto (Jesus) their disciples with the Herodians" (Mt. 22:16). An alliance between the Pharisees and the Herodians has only been seen once before (in Mark 3:6), where again the object was to "destroy Jesus".

Such an alliance is most surprising when the conflicting philosophies of the two parties involved are understood. The Herodians, as their name suggests, were supporters of the family of the Herods, the Hasmoneans. Herod was the leader appointed by the Romans over Israel; but he was not a Jew. The Pharisees had separated themselves from the secular state in Israel. They viewed the Roman rulership and the corruption of the priesthood in its involvement with Herod, as things to be avoided as far as possible. Indeed, the name "Pharisee" is based on the Hebrew *pharez* which means 'divide' – they were not known for being co-operative! Yet they were willing to join up with a group from the opposite end of the political spectrum to bring down Jesus.

The question, "Is it lawful to give tribute unto Caesar, or not?" (Mt. 22:17) was hypocritical, as is evident from their opening flattery ("Master, we know that thou art true, and teachest the way of God in truth, neither carest thou for any man: for thou regardest not the person of men", v. 16). But Jesus sees right through their hypocrisy: "Why tempt ye me, ye hypocrites?" (v. 18). His reply, which focuses on the dual responsibility towards the state and God, silences them to such an extent that they "marvelled, and left him, and went their way" (v. 22).

Both the Pharisees and the Herodians thought that Jesus would fall into the trap which they had combined to set for him, but their own consciences ended up being directly challenged. In just the same way, we are reminded by the Apostle Paul that we too are to "render ... to all their dues" (Rom. 13:7), both by paying taxes as required, and also by giving God the service which is His due.

The second attack on Jesus

Events	Matthew	Mark	Luke	John	Time
Sadducees' question about the resurrection	22:23-33	12:18-27	20:27-40		

Reinforcing the point that these events all happened on the same day, the record continues: "The same day came to him the Sadducees, which say that there is no resurrection, and asked him" (Mt. 22:23). Their attempt to trap Jesus was based on their misunderstanding of Scripture. The Sadducees did not believe in the resurrection of the dead, [2] so their question centred on the absurd situation of a woman who had had seven husbands. What would her position be at the time of the resurrection that Jesus preached?

The Sadducees were Jews who based all their teaching on the first five books of the Bible (*i.e.*, the books of Moses). They were put to silence by Jesus' answer, because it showed, from the books of Moses in which they trusted, that the doctrine of resurrection of the dead was taught there. Jesus referred them to God's interaction with Moses at the burning bush, and asked them:

"… have ye not read that which was spoken *unto you* by God, saying, I am the God of Abraham, and the God of Isaac, and the God of Jacob? God is not the God of the dead, but of the living" (22:31-32).

---

2 "For the Sadducees say that there is no resurrection" (Acts 23:8).

Although spoken about 1500 years earlier, these words, quoted from Exodus 3:6, were addressed not just to Moses, but to the Sadducees also. In this there is a clear warning for us; for whilst neither the Old nor the New Testament was spoken directly to us, they are both of relevance to us in one way or another.

The third attack on Jesus [3]

Events	Matthew	Mark	Luke	John	Time
Which is the great commandment?	22:35-40				
Which is the first commandment?		12:28-34			

Jesus had now dealt with the second onslaught on his authority; but "the contradiction of sinners" against him (Heb. 12:3) was not yet over, for "when the Pharisees had heard that he had put the Sadducees to silence, they were gathered together", in order to ask Jesus their own questions (Mt. 22:34).

Now whilst it may appear that Matthew and Mark are speaking about the same event, a careful consideration of the details contained in the two Gospel records will demonstrate that there were, in fact, two different individuals who asked very similar questions. The question, "Which is the great commandment in the law?" (22:36), seems innocuous enough; but the Spirit informs us that the

---

3 This conclusion is also reached by Bro. Allan Harrison, in 'The First and Great Commandment', *The Christadelphian*, March 1998, p. 91.

one who asked Jesus the question did so "tempting him" (22:35). So even this question must be seen as part of the Jewish leaders' attempts to undermine Jesus' position in the eyes of the people.

Yet once again, Jesus was able to overcome the hostility behind this question. The first and the second commandments, said Jesus, were of twin importance: the first concerned the attitude that men should manifest towards God, and the second was about the attitude that should be manifested towards other men. In bracketing these two commandments together in this way, Jesus skilfully encompassed all aspects of the Law of Moses, as well as all the teaching of Scripture. That is why Jesus was able to conclude: "On these two commandments hang all the law *and the prophets*" (22:40).

The account in Mark 12 recounts the second question on the issue of the commandments. For whereas in Matthew the lawyer asked the question "tempting" Jesus, no such motive is imputed to the scribe in Mark's record. Instead, the scribe's motivation was altogether different from the lawyer's. He had heard that Jesus had "answered them well" (Mk. 12:28). Mark says that the scribe wanted to know more about the commandments in the law – hence his different question: "Which is the first commandment of all?" (Mk. 12:28). The scribe clearly understood the law and the obligations it placed on the faithful believer, for when Jesus responded to him with another carefully worded answer about loving God and our neighbour, the scribe agreed and said:

"Well, Master, thou hast said the truth: for there is one God; and there is none other but He: And to love Him with all the heart, and with all the understanding, and with all the soul, and with all the strength, and to love his neighbour as himself, is more than all whole burnt offerings and sacrifices" (12:32-33).

Far from being hostile to the Lord's teaching, the scribe was told, "Thou art not far from the kingdom of God" (12:34). [4] This conversation with the scribe must have been a great comfort to Jesus during this day of bitter opposition to his authority and teaching.

A comparison of the two records, which speak of the tempting question of the lawyer and the seeking after enlightenment by the scribe, serves to confirm that these were two different, but related, events.

Matthew 22:35-40	Mark 12:28-34
"[35] Then one of them, which was a lawyer, asked him a question, tempting him, and saying, [36] Master, which is the great commandment in the law?	"[28] And one of the scribes came, and having heard them reasoning together, and perceiving that he had answered them well, asked him, Which is the first commandment of all?
[37] Jesus said unto him, Thou shalt love the LORD thy God with all thy heart, and with all thy soul, and with all thy mind. [38] This is the first and great commandment.	[29] And Jesus answered him, The first of all the commandments is, Hear, O Israel; The LORD our God is one LORD: [30] And thou shalt love the LORD thy God with all thy heart, and with all thy soul, and with all thy mind, and with all thy strength: this is the first commandment.
[39] And the second is like unto it, Thou shalt love thy neighbour as thyself. [40] On these two commandments hang all the law and the prophets."	[31] And the second is like, namely this, Thou shalt love thy neighbour as thyself. There is none other commandment greater than these.

4   Luke 10:27 records a lawyer drawing together Deuteronomy 6:5 and Leviticus 19:18 in the same way as Jesus. It is possible that the conjunction of these two verses was not an entirely unusual way of understanding the first and second commandments.

Matthew 22:35-40	Mark 12:28-34
	[32] And the scribe said unto him, Well, Master, thou hast said the truth: for there is one God; and there is none other but he: [33] And to love him with all the heart, and with all the understanding, and with all the soul, and with all the strength, and to love his neighbour as himself, is more than all whole burnt offerings and sacrifices. [34] And when Jesus saw that he answered discreetly, he said unto him, Thou art not far from the kingdom of God. And no man after that durst ask him any question."

Whilst the three questions were all tricks designed to trap Jesus in his words, "no man after that durst ask (Jesus) any question" (Mk. 12:34). If we had been in Jesus' shoes at that time, we might well have taken the opportunity to leave the scene, with the critics silenced. But Jesus was not concerned about himself: he was concerned for the salvation of others. This was why he stayed on to encourage his audience to consider the implications of Scripture, by turning the tables on the leaders with questions of his own.

Jesus questions the leaders

Events	Matthew	Mark	Luke	John	Time
Whose son is Christ?	22:41-46	12:35-37	20:41-44		

By contrast with the leaders' questions, the question Jesus asked "while he taught in the temple" (Mk. 12:35) – "What think ye of Christ? Whose son is he?" (Mt. 22:42) – was not a trick question. It was part of the continual instruction in the Law which Jesus engaged in. Consistent with the three parables which he spoke earlier in the day, Jesus was looking for a response from the leaders. They obliged him with the reply, "The Son of David", to which Jesus posed the further question: "How then doth David in spirit call him Lord ...?" (22:43). But they had no answer to this, and the record tells us that "no man was able to answer him a word, neither durst any man from that day forth ask him any more questions" (22:46). Yet unlike the leaders, the common people "heard (Jesus) gladly" (Mk. 12:37).

Throughout this dialogue, Jesus was directing the religious leaders to the words of Scripture. His objective was to challenge their way of thinking. Their inability to answer Jesus' questions about the meaning of God's Word should have caused them to think again about their understanding. But sadly, the Lord's appeal had no effect – or not at least upon the majority. Rather than acknowledging Jesus' teaching, they saw their interaction with him as a battle. This should cause us to reflect. Do we ever battle against the teaching of Scripture because of our own pre-conceived ideas?

Perceive ye how ye prevail nothing?

At this point in the day John provides details which are not found in the other Gospel records.

Events	Matthew	Mark	Luke	John	Time
We prevail nothing against him				12:19	PM
Greeks came to see Jesus				12:20-26	PM
Now is my soul troubled				12:27-28	PM

Events	Matthew	Mark	Luke	John	Time
A voice as thunder				12:28	PM
Jesus speaks to the people				12:30-36	PM
But though he had done so many miracles ...				12:37-41	PM
Nevertheless some rulers believed				12:42-43	PM
A final appeal				12:44-50	PM

The Lord had finished his public ministry. For three and a half years he had been preaching the kingdom of God. In three days he would be in the sleep of death in the grave. One must wonder at the unbelief of those leaders. But, of course, they had another agenda. Their eyes were blinded, as Isaiah had said, but we must appreciate why they were blind. It was not because they were incapable of seeing the "lamb of God". Their problem was that they did not *want* to see. We learn later that Pilate "knew that the chief priests had delivered him for envy" (Mk. 15:10). This was the self-seeking agenda that the chief priests had set for themselves; and it blinded their eyes so they could not see.

It is important to understand that God does not blind men against their will. Hebrews makes it crystal clear that "without faith it is impossible to please Him: for he that cometh to God must believe that He is, and that He is a rewarder of them that diligently seek Him" (Heb. 11:6). If the leaders had been 'diligently seeking' the lamb of God, they would have been rewarded. But all they were 'diligently seeking' was "the praise of men" (Jno. 12:43). Of course, they did not think that they were seeking the praise of men: they thought that they were worshipping God more effectively than the common people. The Pharisee had been presented by Jesus as praying thus: "I thank thee that I am not as other men are, extortioners, unjust, adulterers, or even as this publican" (Lk. 18:11). It was not even as if their teaching was so astray from what the Lord required. Indeed, Jesus would say, even in the context of a powerful criticism of them, "All therefore whatsoever they bid you observe, that observe and do". But unfortunately, "they (said), and (did) not" (Mt. 23:3).

If all we can learn from the leaders in Jesus' day is that appearances do not necessarily indicate what is going on in a man's heart, we will have learned a lot. In our own worship, it is so easy to slip into the way of thinking that as long as we go to the meeting and greet each other in a brotherly way we are living the gospel. But this can be just a sham. The activities we engage in should be the outworking of what is in our heart. The human mind is always self-seeking. We are no different in our make-up from the religious leaders who crucified the Lord. If we really want to be disciples of Jesus we must understand and apply his uncompromising injunction: "If any man will come after me, let him deny himself, and take up his cross, and follow me" (Mt. 16:24). This can only be achieved by understanding and applying those two commandments singled out by the Lord: love God and love your neighbour.

Now is my soul troubled

So, if Jesus was comforted by the coming of the Greeks (Jno. 12:20-26), why are we told that he said: "Now is my soul troubled; and what shall I say? Father, save me from this hour: but for this cause came I unto this hour" (12:27)? Clearly

Jesus did not want to die. He knew that at the end of his ministry his crucifixion was close at hand. When praying later in Gethsemane he asked that the cup might pass (Mt. 26:39) so we should not be at all surprised that he was concerned about his impending death. Doubtless the crucifixion had played on the mind of Jesus all his life, right from the point in time when he became aware of what would be required of him. But why voice those concerns openly now?

A glimpse into the mind of Paul is seen when he says, "Brethren, my heart's desire and prayer to God for Israel is, that they might be saved" (Rom. 10:1). Likewise, Jeremiah, on three occasions (7:16; 11:14; 14:11), prayed for the people of Judah, even though he had been told that they were to be taken into captivity by the Babylonians. Jeremiah, Jesus and Paul all knew that "The Redeemer" would "come to Zion, and unto them that turn from transgression in Jacob" (Isa. 59:20). And now the Redeemer had come to Jerusalem, but was being rejected by the very people he had come to save. He was being "despised and rejected of men" (53:3). These things affected Jesus as they had affected Jeremiah and would affect Paul. Indeed, the continuing blindness of Israel should affect all who truly love God.

A voice as thunder

It is important to understand and appreciate that Jesus had feelings, like us. He was affected by the things that happened to him and by his interactions with those around him. He was sorrowful (Lk. 18:24); he grieved (Jno. 4:6); he needed to be strengthened (Mt. 4:11; Lk. 22:43); he wept (Jno. 11:35) he was moved with compassion (Mt. 9:36; 14:14; 18:27); he loved (Mk. 10:21). In short, as Hebrews 2:14 says, "Forasmuch … as the children are partakers of flesh and blood, he also himself likewise took part of the same". So the unbelief of the leaders would depress him. If we doubt this – if we think that Jesus was above such things – we have made a Jesus who had no human emotions, and this despite the fact that Hebrews 4:15 categorically states that Jesus is a high priest "touched with the feeling of our infirmities", and who was "in all points tempted like as we are". We must appreciate that Jesus was affected emotionally by his environment. He understood that the same effects were felt by others, and he was able to sympathise with that. He knew, for example, that his disciples would be despondent when he was taken from them. Hence he told them, "I will not leave you comfortless" (Jno. 14:18).

In like manner the Father was aware of the needs of His son. That is why there "came a voice from heaven, saying, I have both glorified it, and will glorify it again" (12:28). The people did not appreciate what was happening, and so those who heard the sound "said that it thundered: others said, An angel spake to him" (12:29). And even though Jesus said, "This voice came not because of me, but for your sakes" (12:30), he will most certainly have received encouragement from hearing his Father's voice of approval.

Jesus speaks to the people

John 12:30-36 is Jesus' last recorded public discourse. In speaking to the multitude (and at the same time also to his disciples – Matthew 23:1), Jesus wades full tilt into the scribes and Pharisees and reproves them (23:1-36). His attention then focuses on the particular needs of his disciples.

In speaking to the people, Jesus returns to the theme of his forthcoming death. In saying, "now shall the prince of this world be cast out", [5] Jesus was trying to make his hearers realise that, despite the way in which his critics had been silenced, their hatred of him would nevertheless culminate in his death. Although he seemed to have a great following at that time, Jesus told the multitude: "And I, if I be lifted up from the earth, will draw all men unto me" (Jno. 12:32). In saying this, Jesus was returning to a topic he raised with Nicodemus when he said: "And as Moses lifted up the serpent in the wilderness, even so must the Son of man be lifted up" (3:14). Nicodemus may have known what Jesus meant, and we certainly do. It is also clear that, even before the crucifixion, the common people understood what was intended by Jesus, for their response was: "We have heard out of the law that Christ abideth for ever: and how sayest thou, The Son of man must be lifted up?" (12:34). They understood that Jesus was saying that he was going to die; and they probably also understood that he was talking about death by crucifixion. But despite the fact that Jesus had been teaching for three years, the common people still did not understand that Messiah was going to conquer sin and death before re-establishing the kingdom of God.

So Jesus' final words to the people were an appeal on moral grounds. His ministry had been one of personal appeal and warning right to the end. He had utilized every opportunity to highlight the need for a response to him and to the love of his Father. In this he is an enduring example to us of perseverance and determination to highlight the love and

---

5 From the three times we meet "the prince of this world" (John 14:30; 16:11 and here) that Jesus is speaking, not of himself, but of that which was the antithesis of everything that he stood for. He was speaking of that power which was the embodiment of sin.

mercy of God for those who will hear and obey while there is still time and opportunity:

> "Yet a little while is the light with you. Walk while ye have the light, lest darkness come upon you: for he that walketh in darkness knoweth not whither he goeth. While ye have light, believe in the light, that ye may be the children of light. These things spake Jesus, and departed, and did hide himself from them" (Jno. 12:35-36).

But though he had done so many miracles

Isaiah had asked: "Who hath believed our report? And to whom is the arm of the LORD revealed?" (Isa. 53:1). Jesus knew the prophets well, so he will not have been surprised at the unbelief of the people. He did not need to wait until the end of his ministry to realise that there would be little response to his message. Isaiah had already instructed him about his hearers by saying that "the LORD hath poured out upon (the children of Israel) the spirit of deep sleep, and hath closed (their) eyes: the prophets and (their) rulers, the seers hath he covered" (29:10). John, quoting this passage, concludes from it: "Therefore they could not believe, because that Esaias said again, He hath blinded their eyes, and hardened their heart; that they should not see with their eyes, nor understand with their heart, and be converted, and I should heal them" (Jno. 12:39-40). So John speaks of the inevitability of the unbelief, saying "they could not believe".

The Son of God had been among them for over three years preaching the gospel, calling for repentance, and working wonders and signs – but his Father had told him already that there would be little or no response to his message. So why did he go through with it? Why did Jesus live a life where he had "not where to lay his head?" (Lk. 9:58), and during which he was willing to suffer such "contradiction of sinners against himself" (Heb. 12:3), even though he knew that there would be only a few who would 'believe his report'? He did it not only because God willed it so and he was obedient, but also as a witness to the Truth of God's unfolding purpose, whether any would believe him or not. And therein lies a valuable twin motivation for our own preaching to our contemporary world.

Nevertheless some rulers believed

But it was not all despair. The record says: "Nevertheless among the chief rulers also many believed on him; but because of the Pharisees they did not confess him, lest they should be put out of the synagogue:" (Jno. 12:42). We can name two of these chief rulers: Nicodemus and Joseph of Arimathea would show their true colours when Jesus was dead.

Jesus "knew what was in man" (2:25); and there were at least two occasions (3:2; 7:50) when Jesus was in the company of Nicodemus. So it is safe to conclude that Jesus was aware of the struggle that was going on in this leader's mind. That knowledge must have been a great comfort to Jesus when it looked as if his work had been in vain (Isa. 49:4).

Beware of the leaders

Events	Matthew	Mark	Luke	John	Time
Woe unto you ... hypocrites	23:1-39	12:38-40	20:45-47		

The refusal by the scribes and Pharisees to consider the implications of Scripture provoked Jesus to say: "Beware of the scribes, which love to go in long clothing, and love salutations in the marketplaces" (Mk. 12:38).

Matthew 23 was spoken just prior to Jesus leaving Jerusalem to go to the Mount of Olives three days before his death. But it was a distillation of what he had already said to the scribes and Pharisees on different occasions beginning with the time of his baptism.

| Events | Parallel accounts | | | | | |
	Matthew 23	Mark 12	Luke 20	Matthew	Mark	Luke
Heavy burdens	v. 4					11:46
To be seen of men	v. 5			6:5		
Uppermost seats	v. 6	v. 39				11:43
Greetings in the market	v. 7		v. 46			11:43
Devour widows' houses	v. 14	v. 40	v. 47			
Make long prayers	v. 14	v. 40	v. 47			
Blind Pharisees	v. 19			15:4		
Tithe	v. 23					11:42
Mercy	v. 23			9:13; 12:7		
Cups and platters	v. 25				7:4	
Whited sepulchres	vv. 27,29					11:47
Generation of vipers	v. 33			3:7; 12:34		3:7
All be fulfilled	v. 36			24:34	13:30	21:32
O Jerusalem	v. 37					13:34

The Lord's major criticism of the scribes and Pharisees focussed on their self-centred lifestyle. They were concerned that what they did would be "seen of men" (Mt. 23:5) They loved the "uppermost seats" (23:6) and "greetings in the market place" (23:7). Even their motivation in prayer was "for a pretence" (23:14). There was an outward show of worship and godliness; but they were busy laying "heavy burdens" on others (23:4), and devouring "widow's houses", no doubt to extend their own (23:14). [6] They made a show of their religion by tithing trivial items (23:23), and making a great show of observing the laws of cleanliness in the way that they washed "cups and platters" (24:26). But they were, in fact, unclean despite this outward show: they were "whited sepulchres" (23:27). They were meticulous in the way in which they observed the letter of the law, taking pride in the traditions that their "fathers" had added to what had been revealed through Moses. Their religion was one of works: they thought that they were pleasing their God by what they did.

A recurring theme in the Scriptures is the fact that God does not really 'want' animal sacrifices. Of course, this is not to be taken to indicate that He did not institute sacrifices. He did; but they were added to remind Israel of their sinfulness, rather than as a means of 'pleasing' Him. God was more interested in what kind of people they were:

"Thus saith the LORD of hosts, the God of Israel; Put your burnt offerings unto your sacrifices, and eat flesh.

---

6 Excavations of this time in Jerusalem highlight that the priests had very comfortable lives. The extensive refurbishment of their houses was underway in the city, even while it was under siege to the Romans. The Herodian villas which have been discovered in the Old City of Jerusalem are a testimony to the words of Jesus.

For I spake not unto your fathers, nor commanded them in the day that I brought them out of the land of Egypt, concerning burnt offerings or sacrifices: But this thing commanded I them, saying, Obey My voice, and I will be your God, and ye shall be My people: and walk ye in all the ways that I have commanded you, that it may be well unto you" (Jer. 7:21-23).

Israel saw the offering of sacrifices as a virtuous end in themselves – they forgot that the offering of a sacrifice was an acknowledgement of their sinfulness, not an opportunity of parading their righteousness. Samuel had to reprove Saul on this point. In direct contravention of God's command, Saul spared the Amalekites, on the flimsy pretext that the people had saved the animals alive to offer as sacrifices to God. Saul, because he did not appreciate the value of obedience, was reproved by Samuel with the words:

"Hath the LORD as great delight in burnt offerings and sacrifices, as in obeying the voice of the LORD? Behold, to obey is better than sacrifice, and to hearken than the fat of rams" (1 Sam. 15:22).

This same principle can also be seen elsewhere in Scripture (for example: Psalm 51:16-17; Proverbs 21:3; Isaiah 1:11-17; Hosea 6:6; Amos 5:21-24). And Jesus reinforced this point by appealing to some of those Scriptures to show that the leaders of his day had also missed the point. Time and again they failed to obey God's words through His prophets and now through His Son:

"O Jerusalem, Jerusalem, thou that killest the prophets, and stonest them which are sent unto thee, how often would I have gathered thy children together, even as a hen gathereth her chickens under her wings, and ye would not! (Mt. 23:37).

This is a very powerful example of the way in which Jesus continually appealed to (and warned) the religious leaders of his day. He made the same point again at this very late stage in his ministry because none of his earlier words to them had been heeded.

Psalm 118 again

Jesus' final words to his detractors were: "Ye shall not see me henceforth, till ye shall say, blessed is he that cometh in the name of the LORD" (23:39). So once again Jesus was drawing the religious leaders' attention to Psalm 118:36. These were the very words that the disciples and the common people had used to welcome Jesus three days previously as he travelled into Jerusalem from Bethany. This was Jesus challenging the leaders to reflect on the real significance of the Psalm and his role as Israel's true Messiah.

So Psalm 118 was used as a focal point of reference on three consecutive days during the week:

Days before the Passover	Events	References	
5	On the way into Jerusalem	Matthew 21:9-10	Psalm 118:25-26
4	When the moneychangers were cast out	Matthew 21:15	Psalm 118:25
3	Did ye never read?	Matthew 21:42	Psalm 118:22
3	Ye will not see me until ...	Matthew 23:39	Psalm 118:26

Of the first occasion when the Psalm was sung (five days before the Passover), we read:

"And when he was come nigh, even now at the descent of the mount of Olives, the whole multitude of the disciples began to rejoice and praise God with a loud voice for all the mighty works that they had seen" (Lk. 19:37).

They "cried, saying, Hosanna; Blessed is he that cometh in the name of the LORD" (Mk. 11:9). "Hosanna" quotes Psalm 118:25 ("save now"), whilst "blessed is he that cometh in the name of the LORD" quotes verse 26. From Luke's account of the 'triumphal entry', we learn that it was not just the people, but "the whole multitude of his _disciples_" who sang the psalm (19:37). So perhaps this incident gives us a little insight into the enthusiasm and expectation of the disciples at that time. The Psalm was habitually sung by Jews at Passover time as they looked for redemption through Messiah – which explains why the religious leaders were so incensed that the people and the disciples were calling out the words of the psalm and applying them to Jesus. And this was also why "some of the Pharisees from among the multitude said unto him, Master, rebuke thy disciples" (19:39).

The following day (four days before the Passover), when Jesus cast out the moneychangers, the people said "Hosanna" (Mt. 21:15), to the renewed displeasure of the chief priests and Pharisees.

The next day (three days before the Passover), Jesus told the parable of the wicked husbandmen (21:33-44). In response to this, the religious leaders condemned themselves by saying, "He will miserably destroy those wicked men, and will let out his vineyard unto other husbandmen, which shall render him the fruits in their seasons" (21:41). Against the background of the triumphal entry into Jerusalem, the repeated use of Psalm 118 is very pointed, especially when Jesus himself asked the leaders:

"Did ye never read in the Scriptures (quoting Psalm 118:22), The stone which the builders rejected, the same is become the head of the corner: this is the LORD's doing, and it is marvellous in our eyes? Therefore say I unto you, the kingdom of God shall be taken from you, and given to a nation bringing forth the fruits thereof" (Mt. 21:42-43).

Three days before the Passover – during which they would have him put to death – Jesus was refocusing their minds on the same Psalm that the common people and the disciples had sung about him as he entered the city two days before.

The leaders have their attention directed to the Psalm again when Jesus, after castigating them for their hypocrisy, says (quoting Psalm 118:26), "Ye shall not see me henceforth, till ye shall say, blessed is he that cometh in the name of the LORD" (Mt. 23:39).

In this way, it can be seen that rather than being 'casual' quotations from the Psalms, there is here a systematic use of Old Testament Scripture, intended to force the leaders to see that Jesus is, indeed, the Messiah spoken of in Psalm 118. Furthermore, by specifically pointing to the phrase "the stone which the builders rejected", Jesus warns the leaders that they are about to reject the man of God's provision. The Messiah was there among them; but he did not fit in to their mould, and so they did not recognise him.

The exhortation is clear. We are looking for Jesus to "appear the second time" (Heb. 9:28). But, through our own perceptions of what we think he should be like, we may not be ready for him. The establishment of the kingdom will be powerful and earth shattering – of that there is no doubt. Yet it is clear from Jesus' teaching that there will be some of his disciples who will not be prepared for it. To those he will say: "Depart from me, ye cursed, into everlasting fire, prepared for the devil and his angels" (Mt. 25:41). The Jewish leaders of Jesus' day thought they were serving God; but they did not recognise Jesus as the Messiah. We might think we are doing God's will; yet we may actually be rejected by our Lord at his appearing. Jesus left the leaders with the words, "*your* house is left unto you desolate" ringing in their ears (23:38). That was the end of his public ministry, and it is important to notice exactly what Jesus said. When he threw out the money changers early in his ministry, he referred to the temple as "*my Father's* house" (Jno. 2:16). But now that same building was "*your* house" (Mt. 23:38). The change was intended to be meaningful.

The undivided attention of the Lord

Jesus now gives his undivided attention to his disciples. He is never seen publicly teaching again from now to the end of the week. His public ministry has ended.

This is one reason why the meal in Bethany was held two days before the Passover, even though Jesus arrived in Bethany six days before the Passover. Jesus knew that he had much to do during the week, but that after the third day before the Passover he would be able to celebrate the raising of Lazarus with the family in Bethany. This will be considered in more detail at the appropriate place in the week.

Jesus in the treasury

Events	Matthew	Mark	Luke	John	Time
The poor widow's gift		12:41-44	21:1-4		Late PM?

As Jesus leaves the temple he pauses by the treasury. He has spoken of the destruction of the temple and all that it stands for. As he sits, he "beheld how the people cast money into the treasury: and many that were rich cast in much" (Mk. 12:41). While he watched, "there came a certain poor widow, and she threw in two mites, which make a farthing" (Mk. 12:42). Jesus tells his disciples: "Verily I say unto you, That this poor widow hath cast more in, than all they which have cast into the treasury" (Mk. 12:43). Her response contrasted starkly with those leaders about whom Jesus had warned the people. But she was oblivious of the eyes of Jesus who understood her generosity.

Jesus' words about the widow and her contribution to the temple may well have triggered the disciples' conversation about "the temple, how it was adorned with goodly stones and gifts" (Lk. 21:5). No doubt the disciples were awed by the magnificence of the building. But Jesus reminds them of what he has already told the religious leaders at least twice: "As for these things which ye behold, the days will come, in the which there shall not be left one stone upon another, that shall not be thrown down" (21:6).

Christ our Passover

That Jesus is "our Passover" (1 Cor. 5:7) is not in doubt – he died at Passover time and was "a lamb without blemish" (1 Pet. 1:19). But in wonderful fulfilment of the details in Exodus 12, even the events of the last week confirm the pattern of Jesus as the Passover lamb, as the following table shows.

Events in Exodus 12	Date in Nisan	Days Before Passover	Events in Jesus' life
Lamb selected: v. 3	10th	5	Enters Jerusalem (Jno. 12:1-2)
	11th	4	Casts out money changers (Mt. 21:12)
	12th	3	Leaders can find no fault (Mt. 22)
	13th	2	Feast in Bethany (Mk. 14:3)
		1	Pilate finds no fault (Lk. 23:4)
Lamb slain: v. 6	14th		Jesus dies (Mk. 15:34)

The lamb was to be selected on the tenth day of the month and kept by the family in the house until it was sacrificed on the fourteenth day of the month. The Jews, during this time, ensured that the lamb was "without blemish" (Exodus 12:5). They did this by examining it to see that it conformed to God's requirements.

Likewise Jesus, during the time that he was in Jerusalem, was 'examined'. He was examined, first, by the religious leaders who, after the onslaught of Matthew 22, were not able to "answer him a word" (v. 46) – Jesus had silenced his Jewish critics; and they had not been able to find any fault in him. Then, during his trial by Pilate, his innocence and his faultless nature were recognized, so that Pilate said, three times, "I find no fault in him" (Jno. 18:38; 19:4,6).

So the Gospel records present Jesus as 'unblemished' as the lamb which was kept by the family from the tenth day of the month Nisan. Both were faultless, and therefore an acceptable sacrifice.

Jesus and his disciples: in the temple and on the way back to Bethany

Events	Matthew	Mark	Luke	John	Time
The poor widow's gift			21:1-4		
The Olivet prophecy	24:1-36	13:1-32	21:5-36		Late PM
Watch, days of Noah	24:37-51				
Ten virgins	25:1-13				
Man travelling into a far country	25:14-31	13:33-37			
Sheep, goats and judgment	25:31-46				

Luke 20:46 provides the summary of the events recorded in Matthew 23, where Jesus reproves the scribes and Pharisees. The final comment that Luke makes is that they "devour widows' houses" (20:47). The language for this comment is drawn from Ezekiel 22:25. Ezekiel has the religious leaders of his day sitting before him and is reproving them for the way they failed to take care of the people, preferring to look after themselves. It is against this background that Ezekiel says:

"There is a conspiracy of her prophets in the midst thereof, like a roaring lion ravening the prey; they have devoured souls; they have taken the treasure and precious things; they have made her many widows in the midst thereof" (Ezek. 22:25).

It is in this kind of context that Luke records how Jesus "saw also a certain poor widow casting in (to the temple treasury) her two mites" (Lk. 21:2). On the one hand, the religious leaders sought to feather their own nests with their ill-gotten gains when they stooped even to the extent of exacting from widows. And yet, of her own free will, and despite the rapaciousness of the leaders, the widow still gave what little she had left. In fact, relatively speaking, she gave more than all of them: "For all these ... of their abundance cast in unto the offerings of God: but she of her penury ... cast in all the living that she had" (Lk. 21:4). [7]

Matthew 24:3 and Mark 13:3 indicate that the disciples were on the Mount of Olives when Jesus gave the prophecy known familiarly as the Olivet Prophecy. So Jesus and the disciples must have walked through the Kidron valley to the Mount of Olives, where they sat down. Jesus then gave the disciples a chilling warning, set out here in the parallel passages:

Matthew 24:2	Mark 13:2	Luke 21:6
"And Jesus said unto them, See ye not all these things? verily I say unto you, There shall not be left here one stone upon another, that shall not be thrown down"	"And Jesus answering said unto him, Seest thou these great buildings? there shall not be left one stone upon another, that shall not be thrown down"	"As for these things which ye behold, the days will come, in the which there shall not be left one stone upon another, that shall not be thrown down"

---

7   We should not allow the division between Chapters 20 and 21 to destroy the thematic flow in Luke's record.

But what is Jesus talking about here? Is he speaking of his second coming, or of the destruction of Jerusalem which happened in AD 70? Matthew and Luke have "these things"; Mark is even more specific, saying "these great buildings". It is difficult to escape the conclusion, therefore, that Jesus is about to tell his disciples what is going to happen to Herod's temple, to which they have drawn his attention. So the *primary* focus of Jesus' attention in the 'Olivet Prophecy' is telling his immediate disciples how the Romans would destroy Herod's temple and preparing them for that event, which would happen in their lifetime.

Matthew and Luke indicate that "the disciples" asked Jesus the question, whereas Mark records more specifically that it was Peter, James, John and Andrew who asked (Mk. 13:3). Why these four should ask together is unclear. All we can say is that these were two sets of brothers: "Simon, who is called Peter, and Andrew his brother; James the son of Zebedee, and John his brother" (Mt. 10:2). Mark and Matthew also tell us that the question was asked "privately".

It is also worth considering *what* the disciples actually asked. Mark and Luke are to all intents and purposes the same. They asked when the things spoken of were going to happen and what would be the sign when these things were to be fulfilled. Matthew, on the other hand, says that the disciples also asked about Jesus' "coming, and the end of the world" (24:3). So what did they mean by "thy coming", since they did not, at that time, fully appreciate that Jesus was going away.

The word translated "coming" in Matthew 24:3 is the Greek word *parousia*. Whilst the word is used in connection with the 'coming' of Jesus, it is not used exclusively of this, nor is it the only word used to speak of Jesus' 'coming'. The table below sets out typical uses of the word *parousia* and the other word (Greek, *erchomai*) which is also translated 'coming'.

New Testament Greek word with translations in KJV & number of occurrences	
parousia ('coming', 22; 'presence', 2)	*erchomai* ('come/coming', 617; 'go', 13; misc., 13)
Matthew 24:27 – "For as the lightning cometh out of the east, and shineth even unto the west; so shall also *the coming* of the Son of man be" (Also vv. 3,37,39)	*Matthew 2:2* – "Where is he that is born King of the Jews? for we have seen his star in the east, and *are come* to worship him" (Also vv. 8-9,11,21,23)
1 Corinthians 15:23 – "But every man in his own order: Christ the firstfruits; afterward they that are Christ's at his *coming*"	*Matthew 24:30* – "And then shall appear the sign of the Son of man in heaven: and then shall all the tribes of the earth mourn, and they shall see the Son of man *coming* in the clouds of heaven with power and great glory"
2 Corinthians 7:6 – "Nevertheless God, that comforteth those that are cast down, comforted us by *the coming* of Titus"	
2 Corinthians 10:10 – "For his letters, say they, are weighty and powerful; but his bodily *presence* is weak, and his speech contemptible"	*Matthew 24:42* – "Watch therefore: for ye know not what hour your Lord *doth come*" (Also vv. 5,39,42-44,46,48)
Philippians 2:12 – "Wherefore, my beloved, as ye have always obeyed, not as in my *presence* only, but now much more in my absence, work out your own salvation with fear and trembling"	*Matthew 25:31* – "When the Son of man *shall come* in his glory, and all the holy angels with him, then shall he sit upon the throne of his glory" (Also vv. 6,10-11,13,19,27,36,39)
1 Thessalonians 2:19 – "For what is our hope, or joy, or crown of rejoicing? Are not even ye in the presence of our Lord Jesus Christ at his *coming*?" (Also 4:15; 5:23; 2 Thess. 2:1,8-9)	*Acts 4:23* – "And being let go, they *went* to their own company, and reported all that the chief priests and elders had said unto them"
2 Peter 3:4 – "And saying, Where is the promise of his *coming*? for since the fathers fell asleep, all things continue as they were from the beginning of the creation"	*Acts 11:12* – "And the Spirit bade me go with them, nothing doubting. Moreover, these six brethren *accompanied* me, and we entered into the man's house"

From the use of the two words, we conclude that there is nothing special, technical, or unusual about the word *parousia*. It is a straightforward word for 'coming', as *erchomai* is a simple word for 'to come'.

"The end of the world" in the disciples' question (in Matthew 24:3) should be understood as the end of an era (*i.e.*, not the end of the earth or of the universe).[8] Jewish thought and Scripture both pointed to a time when Messiah would come and the contemporary order of things would change. The disciples understood Jesus to be the Messiah, so they were expecting the 'consummation of (their) age'. Even after Jesus' resurrection they had the same thought when they asked Jesus: "Wilt thou *at this time* restore again the kingdom to Israel?" (Acts 1:6).

Luke 17 and the Olivet Prophecy

It is difficult to know for certain where Jesus was when he gave the warning about the destruction of Jerusalem recorded in Luke 17:20-37. We do know that the record in Luke from 17:11 to 18:4 is unique to Luke's account. It would appear that it fits into the time period between the raising of Lazarus and the events just prior to Jesus' return to Jerusalem for this third Passover of his ministry. Luke 10:38-42 describes events which took place at the time that Lazarus was raised from the dead.

Luke 17:11 says that Jesus "passed through the midst of Samaria and Galilee", and that the event which immediately preceded this warning was the healing of

---

8   The Greek *synteleias tou aionos* means 'the consummation of the age'.

the ten lepers in that region. Furthermore, Jesus did not arrive in Jerusalem until Luke 19:29, when he came to "Bethphage and Bethany". We can therefore be sure that Luke 17 and the Olivet Prophecy paralleled in Matthew 24, Mark 13 and Luke 21 was spoken on a different occasion from Luke 17:20-37, despite the fact that there are striking similarities between Luke 17 and the Olivet Prophecy. These 'similarities' are shown in the table below, where the words in *underlined italics* are common to Luke, Matthew (and also to Mark 13):

Luke 17	Olivet Prophecy
[20] And when he was demanded of the Pharisees, when the kingdom of God should come, he answered them and said, The kingdom of God cometh not with observation: [21] Neither shall they say, Lo here! or, lo there! for, behold, the kingdom of God is within you. [22] And he said unto the disciples, The days will come, when ye shall desire to see one of the days of the Son of man, and ye shall not see it.	
[23] *And they shall say to you, See here; or, see there: go not after them, nor follow them.*	Matthew 24:26
[24] *For as the lightning, that lighteneth out of the one part under heaven, shineth unto the other part under heaven; so shall also the Son of man be in his day.*	Matthew 24:27
[25] But first must he suffer many things, and be rejected of this generation. [26] *And as it was in the days of Noe, so shall it be also in the days of the Son of man.* [27] *They did eat, they drank, they married wives, they were given in marriage, until the day that Noe entered into the ark, and the flood came, and destroyed them all.* [28] Likewise also as it was in the days of Lot; they did eat, they drank, they bought, they sold, they planted, they builded; [29] But the same day that Lot went out of Sodom it rained fire and brimstone from heaven, and destroyed them all.	Matthew 24:37-39
[30] Even thus shall it be in the day when the Son of man is revealed. [31] *In that day, he which shall be upon the housetop, and his stuff in the house, let him not come down to take it away: and he that is in the field, let him likewise not return back.* [32] Remember Lot's wife.	Matthew 24:17-18

Luke 17	Olivet Prophecy
[33] Whosoever shall seek to save his life shall lose it; and whosoever shall lose his life shall preserve it.	
[34] I tell you, in that night there shall be two men in one bed; the one shall be taken, and the other shall be left.	
[35] *Two women shall be grinding together; the one shall be taken, and the other left.* [36] *Two men shall be in the field; the one shall be taken, and the other left.* [37] And they answered and said unto him, Where, Lord? And he said unto them, *Wheresoever the body is, thither will the eagles be gathered together"*	Matthew 24:28,40-41

Interestingly, there are none of these verbal links between Luke 17 and Luke 21. The account in Luke 17 was spoken specifically to the disciples (Lk. 17:22), even though the Pharisees had asked him a question (17:20); so when Jesus spoke to them again on the Mount of Olives, they had heard a similar message fewer than six months earlier.

The Olivet Prophecy

Whereas the words to the religious leaders were words of judgement, when Jesus spoke to the disciples about the destruction of the temple his concern was very different. When he spoke to the leaders, he told them that the temple was to be destroyed; but when he spoke to his disciples he was concerned for their welfare during the turmoil that was to come.

Jesus placed the emphasis in the prophecy not on the disciples knowing exactly when the destruction of AD 70 was to come; instead, he was concerned that they should be prepared for it when it did come. The warning for the disciples is that at the time of "the end", they would be in extreme danger from those who would seek to overthrow their faith.

Words to the disciples	Matthew	Mark	Luke
Take heed	24:4	13:5	21:8
Deceive	24:5	13:5	21:8
False prophets ... deceive	24:11		
Endure	24:13	13:13	
Deceive/seduce	24:24	13:22	
Told you before	24:25	13:23	
Watch/take heed	24:42	13:33	21:34
Goodman ... watched	24:43		
Be ready	24:44		
Watch therefore	25:13		21:36

Before AD 70 there were those among the believers who questioned the idea that Jerusalem would be destroyed (as in, "Where is the promise of his coming" – 2 Peter 3:4). [9] But the lesson for us from all this is clear. Whilst we do not (nor can we) know the "day nor the hour", we should take care to ensure that we are neither deceived nor become complacent.

A consideration of two parallel passages, from Matthew and Luke (below), shows quite clearly that the immediate focus of Jesus in the Olivet Prophecy is on the events of AD 70 – the destruction of the temple by the Romans. Seen against the background of the two earlier occasions when

---

9   "Coming" here in 2 Peter is *parousia*, as in Matthew 24:3. There is evidence in Peter's letters that when he wrote to the scattered believers, they already had a copy of Matthew's Gospel. So it might be said that Peter is drawing attention to Matthew's Gospel by the use of the word *parousia*.

Jesus warned the religious leaders about the 'desolation' of their 'house', we cannot escape that conclusion:

- *Matthew 24:15* – "When ye therefore shall see *the abomination of desolation*, spoken of by Daniel the prophet, stand in the holy place".
- *Luke 21:20* – "And when ye shall see *Jerusalem compassed with armies*".

Luke explains that, in the context of the destruction of the temple, the "abomination of desolation" (Mt. 24:15; Mk. 13:14) is actually "Jerusalem compassed with armies" (Lk. 21:20). Sudden destruction, coming when people are not aware, is likened to the days of Noah, when men and women were going about their routine daily life, oblivious of the impending flood. In the same way, when the Romans came against Jerusalem, the inhabitants would be busy with their own lives, and would be unconcerned about the impending destruction. [10]

Imminent *and* distant

That the Olivet Prophecy speaks of events that would take place in the lifetime of the disciples is further reinforced by comparing the following extracts, in which the immediate relevance of the message to the disciples is stressed by the use of "ye", "you" and "your':

- "And *ye* shall hear of wars and rumours of wars: see that *ye* be not troubled: for all these things must come to pass, but the end is not yet" (Mt. 24:6).

---

10 For a fuller treatment of the Olivet Prophecy and its fulfilment in AD 70, see: John Allfree, *Our Lord's Olivet Prophecy* (1996).

- "Then shall they deliver *you* up to be afflicted, and shall kill *you*: and *ye* shall be hated of all nations for my name's sake" (Mt. 24:9).

- "When *ye* therefore shall see the abomination of desolation, spoken of by Daniel the prophet, stand in the holy place (whoso readeth, let him understand)" (Mt. 24:15).

- "But pray *ye* that *your* flight be not in the winter, neither on the sabbath day" (Mt. 24:20).

Nevertheless, it should be noted that the prophecy spoke of both immediate and distant events. The use of 'they' in Matthew 24:30 ("And then shall appear the sign of the Son of man in heaven: and then shall all the tribes of the earth mourn, and *they* shall see the Son of man coming in the clouds of heaven with power and great glory") shows that there was to be a fulfilment of at least some of the words that Jesus spoke to the disciples at a time *after* their death.

The warning, however, was first for the disciples who heard the prophecy. The warning of impending judgement, coupled with the apathy of the people, was used by Jesus to warn his disciples: "Watch therefore: for ye know not what hour your Lord doth come" (24:42). And not only were they to watch, but each one of them would need to be "a faithful and wise servant" (24:45).

Behold the fig tree

Luke records that during the Olivet Prophecy Jesus "spake to them a parable; Behold the fig tree, and all the trees" (Lk. 21:29). When this happened, Jesus and his disciples were on the Mount of Olives where, two days earlier, Jesus had been hungry on his way back into Jerusalem from Bethany with his disciples (Mt. 21:18). Finding a fig tree on which there was no fruit, Jesus had cursed it. This time, the next day, as they entered the city, Peter drew attention to the withered fig tree, saying, "Master, behold, the fig tree which thou cursedst is withered away" (Mk. 11:21). So, when Jesus began his parable by repeating Peter's words ("Behold the fig tree"), he was doubtless drawing attention to that same fig tree which he had cursed two days before.

There were, no doubt, other fig trees in the same location, most of them with "nothing but leaves", as the withered one had previously had (11:13). As Jesus said, the disciples knew from the state of the fig trees "that summer (was) now nigh at hand" (Lk. 21:30); but Jesus was leaving them in no doubt, with the object lesson of the withered fig tree, that the destruction of the temple would certainly happen: "So likewise ye, when ye shall see all these things, know that it is near, even at the doors" (Mt. 24:33). The disciples, therefore, would have to live lives separate from the order of things that they had been associated with, because those things were to "vanish away" (Isa. 51:6). Whilst the Jewish order of things seemed stable and certain, it was in fact transient. They were not to place their reliance in the stones of the earthly Jerusalem, but were to look "for a city which hath foundations, whose builder and maker is God" (Heb. 11:10).

It is not good enough to be aware that Jesus is going to come again. The certain knowledge that he is to appear should cause us to be "faithful and wise servants", who will be "found so doing" when he appears (Mt. 24:46). We need to remember that this current order of things will vanish away, despite its apparent permanence.

Yet more parables

Jesus' discourse continues into Matthew 25 with a series of parables, and the chapter division is in an unfortunate position. Chapter 25 was also spoken on the Mount of Olives, and should be seen as a continuation of the 'Olivet Prophecy'. Matthew 24 and 25 are all one single narrative spoken at the same time to the same people; and Jesus' answer to the disciples' original questions ("When shall these things be?" and "What shall be the sign?" – 24:3) was still being given.

The first of these parables, commonly called 'The parable of the ten virgins', addresses both of these elements of the disciples' questions. The conclusion of the parable ("for ye know neither the day nor the hour wherein the Son of man cometh" – 25:13) highlights the fact that the parable relates back to the disciples' questions. Jesus was being careful to warn the disciples against expecting that they could predict *when* the events he had spoken of would take place.

The parable of the ten virgins

This parable, which is unique to Matthew, answers the 'when' of "when shall these things be" (24:3). The focus of the parable is not on a precise time; instead, its focus is on being prepared whenever the time comes.

Whilst half of the virgins were "wise" and half of them were "foolish", we should not infer that only 50% of the disciples would be ready for the events that Jesus had spoken of, or that only 50% of all the believers will be ready for the return of the Lord. The focus is not on *how many* but on "watch therefore" (25:13). When the bridegroom came, "*they all* slumbered and slept" (25:5). All the virgins were asleep, but only half of them were *ready* for the coming of the bridegroom.

The parable draws on the earlier words of Jesus recorded in Luke 13. We have already established that Jesus spoke the words recorded in Luke 13 between the raising of Lazarus and Jesus' arrival in Bethany "six days before the Passover" (Jno. 12:1).

Luke 13	Language	Matthew 25
v. 23	"The door was shut"	v. 10
v. 25	"Lord, Lord, open to us"	v. 11
vv.25, 27	"I know you not"	v. 12

In Luke 13 Jesus exhorts the disciples to "strive to enter in at the strait gate: for many, I say unto you, will seek to enter in, and shall not be able" (Lk. 13:24) He then explained that once the door was shut (13:25), there would be no admission for anyone else, even though they might stand outside crying, "Lord, Lord, open unto us" (Lk. 13:25). Surprisingly, the master would not even acknowledge that he knew them: he is heard to say, "I tell you, I know you not"; and the words are repeated in response to the protestations of those outside (13:27).

In Luke 13:24, the exhortation "strive to enter" itself draws on the even earlier teaching of Jesus. In the Sermon on the Mount Jesus said: "Enter ye in at the strait gate: for wide is the gate, and broad is the way, that leadeth to destruction, and many there be which go in thereat" (Mt. 7:13). So by the time the disciples were sitting with Jesus on the Mount of Olives listening to the parable of the ten virgins, they had heard elements of the words of the parable once a few months before, as well as in the Lord's early seminal discourse. Similarly, the expression "I know you not" (25:12) has its origins in the Sermon on the Mount ("And then will I profess unto them, I never knew you" – Matthew 7:23). The parable of the ten virgins is therefore a bringing together of elements from the Sermon on the Mount and the exhortation in Luke 13:24-30.

Travelling into a far country

The second parable is about a man travelling into a far country. Mark 13 contains a very shortened version of the parable, while Matthew 25 has a longer record of it. The 'talents' were distributed "to every man according to his several ability" (Mt. 25:15); so we have to conclude that each of the servants could have 'traded' in a way which would have been acceptable to the master. Two of the servants gained from their trading. The third was rejected by his master because of his attitude in not keeping his lord's instruction to 'trade' with what he had been given. Jesus puts into his mouth some of the words that Adam spoke to God in Eden after the Fall: "*I was afraid* and went *and hid* thy talent" (25:25). [11] This confirms that the servant knew that he had done wrong by not trading, just as Adam knew that he had failed to keep God's commandment. The lesson of the parable is that disciples must not think of their heavenly Father as an overbearing God who lacks compassion.

The sheep and the goats

The third parable taught the disciples that their superficial observation of others was an insufficient basis for judging

---

11 The *italic text* represents the words of Adam in Genesis 3:10.

who was, or was not, doing the Father's will. The dividing of "sheep from the goats" (25:32) demonstrates this. Whilst we might think that the difference between sheep and goats is easy to tell, this is not necessarily so in Israel. There are strains of sheep and goats which are very similar in appearance. In the parable, the difference between the sheep and the goats was not to be discerned by looking on the outward appearance. Instead, it consisted of the way that the people represented by the sheep and the goats responded to others. The sheep cared for others and did things "as unto Christ" (Eph. 6:5). The 'goat class' were selfish and gave no thought to others.

It should not be thought that the placing of the sheep on the right and the goats on the left was an arbitrary choice. The right hand was a place of honour. Hence Jesus himself is now sitting on the right hand of God (Ps. 110:1). This is why the Preacher, by the Spirit, teaches us that "A wise man's heart is at his right hand; but a fool's heart at his left" (Eccl. 10:2). The sheep were placed on the right because they were "wise". The faithful disciple of Jesus manifests his love for his master by showing his love to others; for "If a man say, I love God, and hateth his brother, he is a liar: for he that loveth not his brother whom he hath seen, how can he love God whom he hath not seen?" (1 Jno. 4:20).

Lessons for disciples

Combining the three parables which Jesus told in response to the disciples' questions, we see that Jesus warned them against expecting his immediate return, and that he counselled them to work for him in his absence and to manifest their love for him in their dealings with others. Taken together with his warnings to 'watch' and 'take heed' (Mt. 24), it is clear that Jesus did far more than just foretell the destruction of Jerusalem and his own eventual reappearance. Directed at the disciples, the 'Olivet Prophecy' anticipated the disciples' problems, and the focus of Jesus' teaching moved on from criticising and warning the religious leaders to preparing his disciples for his death.

The Lord's messages to his first-century followers are personally relevant for us today. If we focus simply on Jesus' prediction of the overthrow of Jerusalem and his future appearing, we will miss much of the Lord's concern for his disciples. We might even find ourselves numbered among the foolish virgins, be judged a 'goat', or be rejected as a 'wicked servant'.

Isaiah 5 and the third day before the Passover

This third day before the Passover occupies a large part of the Gospel records of the last week of Jesus' mortal life. For example, the events of Matthew 21–25 all took place on a single day. It is remarkable, too, that the language of Isaiah's fifth chapter features right across Matthew and Luke's record of this third day, as the table below illustrates:

Isaiah	Language	Gospel record
5:2	vineyard … winepress therein	Matthew 21:33
5:5	break down wall	Luke 21:6
5:5	trodden down	Luke 21:24
5:8,11,18,20-22	woe	Matthew 23:13-16, 23,25,27,29

The simple explanation for this use of the language of Isaiah 5 by the Spirit in Matthew 21 and 23 and Luke 21 lies in the identical contexts of Isaiah's prophesying and the Lord's dealings with his enemies. In Isaiah 5 the prophet condemns the sinfulness of the religious leaders, the parable of the vineyard at the beginning of Isaiah 5 speaks of "The house of Israel" (5:7), and the chapter then catalogues some of the leaders' sins. They had no regard for inheritance (5:8); they substituted God's righteous laws for their own traditions (5:20); and they took bribes (5:23). These were some of the reasons for them suffering "the anger of the LORD" (5:25).

In similar fashion, the Lord Jesus, when he arrived in the city of Jerusalem, was confronted by the religious leaders who questioned his authority to speak on behalf of God (Mt. 21:23). They were unwilling also to acknowledge the authority of John the Baptist; and by his use of parables, Jesus went right to the root of their opposition to his message by showing that, unlike John, they were not doing the Father's will. Matthew 21:28-32 challenged them with the question about the two sons and which of them did their father's will. Matthew 21:33-42 applied Isaiah's parable about the vineyard; and this represents the first time that Jesus used Isaiah 5 in his ministry. The leaders, who would no doubt know their Scriptures, realised that Jesus "spake of them" (21:45).

Later in the day, "no man was able to answer him a word" (21:46) after he had challenged their understanding of Psalm 110. This was the second time during this same day that they had been unable to answer his questions. The first was when he asked them about John the Baptist; and, having silenced his critics, he reminded the common people of the status of the "scribes and Pharisees" (23:2), roundly condemning them for their hypocrisy. The repeated use of the word "woe" reflects the same usage in Isaiah 5. There are only two other chapters in Scripture where "woe" is as concentrated as we find it in Matthew 23: Isaiah 5 and Habakkuk 2. The latter speaks about the Babylonian invasion (1:6), which is a pattern of the destruction of Jerusalem by the Romans in AD 70. Given the earlier use of Isaiah 5 to develop the parable of the vineyard which the leaders perceived was directed at them, it is inconceivable to think that they did not also recognise this repeated use of "woe" as speaking of the destruction that awaited them imminently for their wrongdoing.

Jesus' final appeal to Isaiah 5 occurred during his discourse on the Mount of Olives (Mt. 24/Mk. 13/Lk. 21). Having left the temple, Jesus was now speaking to his disciples, to warn them about the impending destruction of Jerusalem and its temple. Isaiah 5 spoke of the destruction of the vineyard as the consequence of the rebellion of the religious leaders, while Jesus left the religious leaders with the awful words "Your house is left unto you desolate" (Mt. 23:38). The Lord's words to the disciples on the Mount of Olives provided further confirmation of this judgement.

Summary of the third day before the Passover

This is the longest day in the last week of Jesus' life: there is more recorded about this day than any other, with the possible exception of the day of the Crucifixion.

The day commences, according to the Gospel records, with the disciples seeing the withered fig tree that Jesus had cursed the day before. This fig tree is highlighted again in the Olivet Prophecy towards the end of this day.

On arriving in the temple Jesus is challenged about his cleansing of the temple the previous day. Focus is made on the baptism of John which silences Jesus' critics.

What follows is a threefold attack on Jesus' position which he silences. The only positive reaction that he receives at this time are the thoughts and question of the scribe who heard that Jesus had answered the lawyer "well". Jesus uses the opportunity to challenge his critics with a question about Christ which confounded his critics. Jesus then speaks to the leaders in parables, showing them that God would destroy the temple because of their wickedness. He follows this up with a stinging criticism of the scribes and Pharisees. This ends his public ministry, so to speak. From now on the Gospels focus on Jesus' care for his disciples.

The Olivet Prophecy is given to warn the disciples about the events which are to come upon Jerusalem and its inhabitants. A number of parables are built into the prophecy to reinforce the warnings.

Chapter 6:
Two days before the Passover

Events	Matthew	Mark	Luke	John	Time
Sanhedrin plot to kill Jesus	26:1-5	14:1-2	22:1-2		AM
The meal in Bethany	26:6-13	14:3-9		12:2-3	Eve
Mary anoints Jesus for his burial	26:6-13	14:3-9		12:2-8	Eve
Judas agrees to betray Jesus	26:14-16	14:10-11	22:3-6		Eve

The next two days have one thing in common: we know very little about what took place during each day. The Gospels concentrate on the events in the evening. This is rather like the fifth day before the Passover, which was the day on which there was the 'triumphal entry' into Jerusalem. On that day we learn about the entry into Jerusalem, which was but one small fragment of the day.

The main focus of this day, two days before the Passover, is the meal in Bethany. The only other event recorded is the Sanhedrin plot to kill Jesus. Thus, even though that event is recorded, it actually tells us nothing about what Jesus himself did; it simply sets the scene for the actions of Judas in the evening, when he goes to the chief priests.

It may appear, on a first reading of John 12:1-2 ("Then Jesus six days before the Passover came to Bethany ... There they made him a supper"), that the "supper" referred to by John was held *six* days before the Passover. But both Matthew (26:2,6) and Mark (14:1,3) place the meal in Bethany *two* days before the Passover; and if we prefer to argue that John is speaking of a meal six days before the Passover, then we have to accept one of the following conclusions:

1. There were two suppers in Bethany in the last week of Jesus' life (on days 6 and 2 before the Passover) and Jesus was anointed with precious ointment by a woman on both occasions;

2. Either John or Matthew and Mark were mistaken about the day on which this supper took place; or,

3. Matthew and Mark have the event out of chronological sequence for some unexplained reason.

Actually, the logical conclusion to be drawn is that all the Gospel writers are speaking about the same meal, and that it took place two days before the Passover. The apparent differences between the accounts are a consequence of the objectives of each inspired writer.

It is possible to develop a detailed table which shows similarities between the meal in Bethany as recorded in John and the one recorded in Matthew and Mark. These similarities can be taken to suggest quite strongly that one event is spoken of. On the other hand, it is possible to develop a detailed table which highlights the differences between John, on the one hand, and Matthew and Mark on the other; and this exercise serves to indicate that the meal spoken of by John is a different meal from the one spoken of by Matthew and Mark. Again, it is also possible to compare the record in Matthew with the one in Mark and find both differences and similarities, and the conclusion might be reached that there was one meal, or perhaps two!

But such an approach is futile. It presumes that similarities or differences between different accounts can, of themselves, 'prove' whether two accounts speak of the same event or not. This approach is futile because it runs the risk of missing the important point that each writer, by the Spirit, had clear objectives in mind. The reader should be looking for themes in the Gospels which explain why each record is as it is. This is supremely relevant when considering the meal at Bethany.

The Bethany supper seems to have been held to celebrate the raising of Lazarus, and we should read John 12 with this in mind. John 12:1 fixes the day of Jesus' arrival in Bethany and therefore enables us to draw the conclusions we have been making about timing throughout the rest of the week. But John 12:2-11 is an account of events which took place two days before the Passover. They are placed here, in parenthesis, because they link thematically with the events recorded in John 11, before Jesus went to "a city called Ephraim" (John 11:54).

That the meal was held two days before the Passover even though Jesus arrived in Bethany six days before the Passover may relate to Jesus' workload during the week. Consider the following:

Jesus' arrival in Bethany six days before the Passover would not be heralded by a phone call to the family there! Jesus' arrival would be, probably, an unexpected and pleasant surprise. The raising of their brother Lazarus would still be very much in the minds of Mary and Martha and his father Simon. Jesus had left Bethany in rather a hurry after the raising of Lazarus because of the plot to kill him (Jno. 11:53). But now, the family might have thought that it would be a good time to have a meal together to celebrate this event. After all, Passover was a joyful time of the year.

The Passover was to be celebrated in six days. The family in Bethany was totally unaware of what was going to happen during the week and the work that Jesus had to do before his crucifixion. Jesus, on the other hand, knew that he had much to do, but that he would finish the work with the religious leaders part way through the week, and that thereafter he would be able to focus specifically on the needs of his disciples. Knowing this, he may well have responded to the enthusiastic and loving offer of a celebratory supper in the house of Lazarus in Bethany by suggesting that it be postponed until two days before the Passover.

The anointing of Jesus

When the alabaster box was broken, "the house was filled with the odour of the ointment" (Jno. 12:3). Although we do not see a house being filled with an odour elsewhere in Scripture, the concept of a house being filled is seen in a number of places in Scripture. 1 Kings 8:10-11 and 2 Chronicles 5:13-14 speak of the glory of God filling Solomon's temple. It was seen in the cloud which filled the temple. When Solomon, at the dedication of the temple, finished praying, the glory of God filled the temple (2 Chron. 7:1-2). When Ezekiel, in vision, witnessed the destruction of Solomon's temple by the Babylonians, he saw the glory of

God as it filled the house of God before it departed from the city (Ezek. 10:3-4). When God says, through Haggai (2:7), "I will fill this house with glory", He is looking to the time when the temple which Ezekiel describes is built once again. The New Testament introduces the idea of the house being filled (Jno. 12:3) in the context of the burial of Jesus, and the link between Jesus' death and the manifestation of God's glory in the house can be seen. The "house" of which we speak is, in fact, the ecclesia, "for ye are the temple of the living God" (2 Cor. 6:16). It is fitting, therefore, that "there came a sound from heaven as of a rushing mighty wind, and it filled all the house" (Acts 2:2). This contrasts starkly with the mentality of the sinner who would entice the son to "fill his house with spoil" (Prov. 1:13) – rather like Judas who, when the house in Bethany was filled with the odour of ointment, went to the chief priests, greedy for "the reward of iniquity" (Acts 1:18).

Dead flies

"Dead flies cause the ointment of the apothecary to send forth a stinking savour" (Eccl. 10:1). This is not simply a comment on the way in which perfume can be spoiled through contamination. Ecclesiastes is using it as a parable, for the verse continues: "… so doth a little folly him that is in reputation for wisdom and honour" (10:1). A Biblical example will serve to demonstrate the truth of the whole parable, which provides a lesson for our own lives.

Judas Iscariot was one who was "in reputation for wisdom and honour". He "had the bag" (Jno. 12:6) – a responsible job and a position of trust. But his 'honour' proved to be undeserved: it was just a "reputation", because he was, in fact, "a thief" (12:6). It was because he was a thief that he was motivated to ask: "Why was not this ointment sold for two hundred pence and given to the poor?" (12:5). Judas was like the "dead flies" of Ecclesiastes 10. His reaction to the use of the ointment on Jesus was the "stinking savour" (Eccl. 10:1). This is because, as John informs us, it was Judas who raised the criticism. Matthew presents the development of the criticism by saying that "they (the disciples) had indignation saying, To what purpose was this waste?" (Mt. 26:8) – although Mark records that these thoughts were "within themselves" rather than openly expressed (14:4). Judas voiced the words, and in so doing caused the other disciples to start thinking evil thoughts. The meal, which had been arranged to celebrate the raising of Lazarus (Jno. 11), was soured by Judas 'dead fly' behaviour. Just as a small amount of corruption spoils the beautiful aroma of the perfume of the apothecary, so one person was able to destroy the joy and harmony of the meal in Bethany. As the "room was filled with the odour of the ointment" (Jno. 12:3), so the 'dead fly' began his evil work of corruption. "Then one of the twelve, Judas Iscariot, went unto the chief priests" (Mt. 25:14). Judas, although he was "in reputation", was not at one with Jesus and the other disciples. He was self-seeking. The meal in Bethany provided the environment where his true colours showed. He was one of those of whom John later wrote that "they went out from us but they were not of us" (1 Jno. 2:19).

The "fool" of Ecclesiastes has his heart "at his left" (Eccl. 10:2) whereas the wise man's is "at his right hand" (10:12). This not an anatomical comment (!) but a marker of spirituality, and a determinator at the judgement, for it is those who are "on (the Master's) right hand" (Mt. 25:34) who will inherit the blessing, whereas those "on the left hand" (25:41) will not. So where is our heart? Are we "dead flies"? Are the thoughts of our hearts corrupting ourselves and others? Will we be among those to whom the Lord says, "Depart from me ye cursed" (25:41)?

Chronological or thematic?

One issue which has exercised Bible students for a long time is 'Did Mary anoint Jesus' head, his feet, or both his head and his feet?' The question is raised because of the way in which the Gospel records present information about the event. But consider the three accounts of the anointing of Jesus in Bethany:

- *Matthew 26:7* – "poured it on his head"

- *Mark 14:3* – "poured it on his head"

- *John 12:3* – "anointed the feet of Jesus"

The apparent anomaly is resolved by taking into account the approach which each writer is developing through the Spirit. We should not make our focus the superficial _differences_ between the records as if this is the major issue. We should appreciate that each writer was moved by the Holy Spirit to develop his record in a particular way. It is naive to conclude that the differences indicate problems with inspiration. Differences in Scripture between parallel accounts require careful examination as the differences often indicate detailed themes, with each writer using specific unique words and ideas as part of their inspired themes. So here, the synoptic Gospel writers, Matthew and Mark, make a particular mention of the head of Jesus being anointed, no doubt because that is where the anointing began. John, on the other hand, picks out the subsequent stage of the anointing – on Jesus' feet – because (as we shall see), John makes 'feet' a theme; and the thematic approach is a feature of John's Gospel throughout.

Consider also the following passages:

- *Matthew 26:6* – "Now when Jesus was in Bethany, in the house of Simon the leper".

- *John 12:4* – "… then one of his disciples, Judas Iscariot, Simon's son".

- *Matthew 26:2* mentions "two days before the Passover". Jesus was in the house of Simon the leper when a woman came with a box of ointment and poured it on his head.

- *John 12:1* records events commencing "six days before the Passover". Sometime subsequent to that Jesus was at a meal which "they" made for him. The context is a house in Bethany where Martha served (vv. 1-2). If Martha was making the meal, it would seem reasonable that she was in her own home. We know that she lived in Bethany because Lazarus was her brother and he lived in Bethany (Jno. 11:1-2).

- *Matthew 26 and John 12* are speaking of the same event. Both records are recounting events just prior to Jesus' death, and they have Jesus in the same place. Matthew 26 speaks of "two days before the Passover", whilst John 12 has "six days". This is because Matthew is presenting a chronological account whilst John's record is thematic. The meal and the anointing of Jesus are linked thematically with the raising of Lazarus, which is recorded in the previous chapter (John 11). John's record links the raising of Lazarus with the meal to show that the meal was a celebration of Lazarus' resurrection.

Additionally, Matthew deals with a series of events in the last week, and speaks of "two days before the Passover" in its chronological sequence. John, on the other hand, provides little information about events between the arrival of Jesus in Bethany, "six days before the Passover", and the celebratory meal two days before the Feast. In fact, rather than concentrating on any particular events during that period, John spends a great deal of time recording what happened in the upper room (Jno. 13-17).

The family of Lazarus: who was related to whom?

The following points help us to work out some of the family relationships:

1. Lazarus was the brother of Mary and Martha.
2. Judas' father was called Simon.
3. Mary and Martha's father was Simon the leper.
4. Simon and Simon the leper were probably the same person.
5. Mary, Martha and Lazarus lived in Bethany.
6. Simon the Leper was Judas' father.
7. Therefore Mary and Martha were sisters to both Lazarus and Judas Iscariot.

It might be observed that 'Simon' was a common name in first-century Israel. But there is a detail in John's account which serves to support the suggestion that Simon the leper was Judas' father. Writing about the meal in Bethany, John calls Judas Iscariot "Simon's son" (12:6). The only 'Simon' mentioned in the context of this meal is "Simon the leper" (Mt. 26:2; Mk. 14:3). Whilst the appellations "Simon the leper" and "Simon's son" are found in different Gospels, we see this as presumptive evidence that the "Simon" who was Judas' father was the same 'Simon' in whose house the supper was held.

A family tree of those in Simon's house in Bethany might look like this:

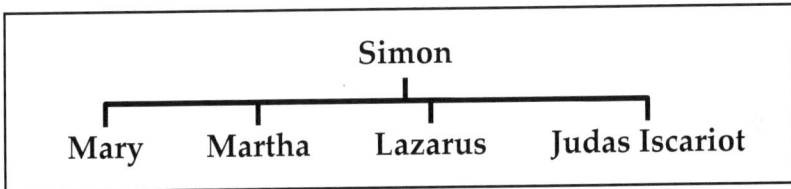

```
                        Simon
        ┌──────────┬──────┴──────┬──────────────┐
      Mary      Martha        Lazarus      Judas Iscariot
```

The suggestion that Judas was the brother of Lazarus provides a possible explanation for Judas' behaviour. For three-and-a-half years Judas had "companied" (Acts 1:21) with Jesus. There is no record that Jesus made any special provision or had any celebration for him. On the other hand, Lazarus, who appears on the scene from nowhere, received a great deal of attention from Jesus at this time. Judas, it is suggested, may have felt pushed out by his brother, who was getting all the attention. Even his sisters, Mary and Martha, were paying more attention to Jesus and (probably) Lazarus than they were to him.

We know that Judas was a thief (Jno. 12:6); and it may have been this, coupled with his sullenness at being upstaged, from his own viewpoint at least, by his brother Lazarus which prompted his action. Judas was jealous. Maybe also he was upset at having been so openly rebuked by Jesus, after Judas had asked, "Why was not this ointment sold for three hundred pence, and given to the poor?" (Jno. 12:5).

It has already been suggested that the unique section in Luke which includes the parable of the prodigal son was spoken by Jesus while he was in "a city called Ephraim" (Jno. 11:54). This places that parable between the raising of Lazarus and the meal in Bethany two days before the Passover. If Judas and Lazarus were indeed brothers in the flesh, then the parable of the prodigal (Lk. 15:11-32) might take on added significance, since Jesus develops the parable's lesson by contrasting the behaviour of two brothers. The prodigal son wasted his share of the inheritance but was welcomed home warmly by the father, whereas the elder son remained with his father all the time his brother was away squandering his share of the inheritance. The setting and the language that Jesus puts into the mouth of the father echo some of the details of the raising of Lazarus, and they are echoed in aspects of Judas' behaviour at the meal in Bethany.

Parable of the prodigal in Luke	Lazarus	The meal in Bethany
15:11 – two sons		John 12:2 – Lazarus and Judas both there (two sons)
15:23 – Make merry because dead son is alive	Restored to the family	The reason for the meal in Bethany
15:28 – Elder son would not go into the feast		Matthew 26:14 – Judas went out of the meal
15:24 – dead/alive	John 11:44 – Lazarus raised from the dead	
15:28 – brother angry		John 12:4 – Judas angry
15:32 – this thy brother	Judas and Lazarus brothers	Judas and Lazarus brothers

The parable of the prodigal son was spoken after the raising of Lazarus (and before the meal in Bethany) by Jesus, who "needed not that any should testify of man: for he knew what was in man" (Jno. 2:25). Jesus "knew from the beginning who they were that believed not, and who should betray him" (6:64). We are entitled, therefore, to see the parable of the prodigal son as an exhortation to Judas, against the background of the raising of Lazarus. Jesus, anticipating what was in Judas' mind, attempted to instruct him to repent and to change the way he thought about himself. The supper in Bethany, two days before the Passover, demonstrated how Judas was so like the elder brother who would not go into the feast.

John 12:2-11 – an inspired digression

John is the only Gospel writer who records the raising of Lazarus. He is also the only one to tell us that Lazarus was at the meal in Bethany ("Lazarus was one of them that sat at the table with (Jesus)" – 12:2). A further link between the raising of Lazarus (in John 11) and John's account of the meal in Bethany is the mention by name of Martha and Mary (12:2-3), whilst, by contrast, neither woman is named in Matthew 26 or Mark 14. So John places the account of the meal at Jesus' point of entry into Bethany because of the thematic link he is making with the raising of Lazarus in his previous chapter.

With this in mind, a consideration of John 12:1-12 will enable us to conclude that the reference to "six days before the Passover" is a marker as to when Jesus arrived in Bethany. The account of the meal is included, but is effectively placed in parenthesis because of the thematic link with the previous chapter. Matthew and Mark, on the other hand, describe the meal where it occurred chronologically, as they had no reason to recount it elsewhere. In other words, the 'harmonisation' of John 12 with Matthew 26 and Mark 14 involves seeing John 12:2-11 as a digression, or a placeholder. The 'chronological' way to read John would be to pass from John 12:1 directly to John 12:12.

John has already digressed in a similar way when speaking of the raising of Lazarus. The section in italics below, for example, is an earlier case of digression in John's Gospel:

> "Now a certain man was sick, named Lazarus, of Bethany, the town of Mary and her sister Martha. *It was that Mary which anointed the Lord with ointment, and wiped his feet with her hair, whose brother Lazarus was sick*" (11:1-2).

Whichever Gospel record we review, it is clear that the raising of Lazarus occurred *before* Jesus was anointed in Bethany. This is evidence in itself to support the view that John uses digression in his Gospel.

The conclusion that John 12:2-11 is a digression enables us to read John in a way which makes it consistent with Matthew 26 and Mark 14. But the realisation that John is structured differently in order to create a thematic link between the raising of Lazarus and the meal in Bethany, is 'simply' one of the many rewarding outcomes of Bible study. It is also an encouragement to probe a little further into the text of Scripture to try to understand John's inspired approach to the events recorded.

Two suppers: in Bethany and in the upper room in Jerusalem

Our study shows clearly that the meal in Bethany and the meal in the upper room, which we call 'The Last Supper', took place on consecutive evenings. The meal in Bethany was to celebrate the raising of Lazarus, whilst the meal in the upper room was to (pre-)memorialise Jesus' death. There are striking parallels between the two meals:

Reference	Two days before the Passover Bethany meal event	One day before the Passover Upper Room supper event	Reference
	Jesus with his friends	*Jesus with his disciples*	
John 12:1	Disciples present	Disciples = 'his friends'	John 15:4
John 12:2	Martha served	Jesus served	Luke 22:27
Matthew 26:7	Poured	"poureth"	John 13:5
John 12:3	Wiped his feet	Wash (wiped) ... feet	John 13:5
John 12:4	Should betray	One will betray	Matthew 26:21
John 12:7	Day of burying	Blood ... shed	Matthew 26:28
John 12:10	Consulted to kill Lazarus	Counsel to kill Jesus	John 11:53
Mark 14:10	Judas went out	Judas went out	John 13:30
John 12:11	Many believed on Jesus (because of raising of Lazarus)	Many believed on him (because of raising of Lazarus)	John 12:42

These similarities are interesting; but 'So what?' – we must be able to benefit from what we see.

The raising of Lazarus incited many to believe on Jesus (John 12:11). This 'belief' extended to the "chief rulers", of whom "many believed" (12:42), although on both occasions the leaders wanted to kill both Lazarus (12:10) and Jesus (11:53). But as noted above, the leaders failed to take action because "they feared the people" (Mk. 12:12).

This was the behaviour of people unwilling to live a life consistent with their beliefs. We can be just the same: we may see a situation in ecclesial life about which we ought to speak up. But we keep silent because we are concerned what others may think of us, and how they might react to what we say.

The two meals were both intimate events. On both occasions, Jesus and his friends and various family members were together. We can imagine the warmth at the meal in Bethany. Jesus and the disciples had endured a tiring three days in Jerusalem. The friendship and warmth of that family in Bethany would have been a pleasant respite from the barbs and deceit of Jesus' opponents. He was among friends, and there will have been no threat there.

The following night, in the upper room, he was with his friends – the disciples. Although there was some rivalry between them as to who was to be the greatest in the Kingdom (Lk. 22:24), there was no open hostility to Jesus, as there had been in the city during the days leading up to the meal in Bethany. Even though the disciples did not know what was going to happen to their Lord, and were puzzled about some of the things that he said, they bore him no animosity.

And yet, at both intimate meals a betrayer was present – in Bethany (Jno. 12:4; Mt. 26:14), and in the upper room (Mt. 26:21-25). The behaviour of Judas on both occasions demonstrated that he did not want to be with Jesus. His mind and heart were elsewhere. When he left the meal in Bethany to go to the chief priests in Jerusalem, he walked some three miles, in the dark, into the city – that is how unhappy he was about the "waste" of the ointment in Bethany.[1]

By contrast to Judas, who presented his concern as being "for the poor" (Jno. 12:5), the woman anointed Jesus' feet because of her love for him. The cost of the ointment was not an issue for her. Her response, by contrast to the reaction of Judas, focused on Jesus rather than on herself. We learn of Judas' motives when we read: "This he said, not that he cared for the poor; but because he was a thief, and had the bag, and bare what was put therein" (12:6). Mary's thoughts were totally different, for Jesus tells us that "against the day of my burying hath she kept this ointment" (12:7).

Summary of the second day before the Passover

We learn little about Jesus' daytime activities during this period. The record focuses on the meal in Bethany, held to celebrate the raising of Lazarus from the dead.

The anointing of Jesus in Bethany and the washing of the disciples' feet in the upper room have striking similarities. Likewise, the behaviour of Judas on both occasions is a powerful warning. During both meals he "went out" because he preferred his own plans to the fellowship of Jesus and his disciples. Lessons about ourselves are clear: we can be like Judas in our life in Christ.

---

1 The issue of Judas' departure from 'The Last Supper' is discussed in the next chapter, "The same night in which he was betrayed ..." on page 145.

Chapter 7:
One day before the Passover

Overview of the day

Events	Matthew	Mark	Luke	John	Time
Preparation for the Passover meal [1]	26:17-20	14:12-17	22:7-14		AM

---

1 The following paragraphs are quoted from John Henry Blunt, *Dictionary of doctrinal and historical Theology* (Longmans, new edition, 1892), p. 543: "Various difficulties have surrounded the reckoning of Easter from the first origin of the Christian Church. The three synoptic Gospels are unanimous … in their statement that our Lord instituted the Holy Eucharist at his last Paschal Supper … John is equally precise in saying that the Jews would not enter the judgment hall "lest they should be defiled" through blood pollution, and be precluded from eating the Passover in the evening (John 18:28). How came it then that our Lord should have celebrated the Passover on one evening and that the Jews should have deferred the memorial feast till the corresponding period of the next day? This is a real difficulty, but the following is probably the solution.

Since the appearing of the new moon determined the Jewish calendar, an assembly was held in the Temple, on the closing day of each month, to receive intelligence respecting the sighting of the new moon. If nothing was announced, a day was intercalated; yet if the appearance of the moon was afterwards authenticated

Events	Matthew	Mark	Luke	John	Time
Disciples strive about "who is the greatest?"			22:24-30		Eve
Jesus washes the disciples' feet				13:1-20	Eve
Identification of Jesus' betrayer	26:21-25	14:18-21	22:21-23	13:21-30	Eve
Memorial meal instituted	26:26-29	14:22-25	22:15-20		Eve
Judas leaves				13:30	Night
A new commandment I give you				13:31-35	Night
Prediction of Peter's denial	26:31-35	14:27-31	22:31-38	13:36-38	Night
Discourses in the Upper Room				14:1-31	Night
Then they sang a hymn	26:30	14:26			

the intercalation was cancelled. This naturally caused much confusion, especially in the critical month of Nisan. Hence (Talmud, Rosh Hashanah Gem. 1) it was permitted that in doubtful cases the Passover might be observed on two consecutive days. For the intercalation of a day at Jerusalem could hardly be known in Galilee; and according to Maimonides, in these more distant parts of Judaea, the Passover was in some years kept one day, at Jerusalem on another. Our Lord coming in from the country followed the letter of the Law, but the main body of the Jews, observing the "tradition of the elders", sacrificed the Passover on the following day, in consequence of the intercalation of a day in the preceding month. Thus our Lord ate the Passover on the evening of the 14th Nisan, and was upon the same day the 'very Paschal Lamb' by the death of the cross."

Events	Matthew	Mark	Luke	John	Time
Then they leave the Upper Room				14:31	
Cross the Kidron				18:1	
Gethsemane/Olives	26:20	14:26	22:39		

This day, like the previous day, is one about which we
are told very little regarding the activities of Jesus and the
disciples during the daylight hours. All we learn about the
events of the daytime is that the disciples went to make
ready for the evening meal. As with the day before, the
emphasis is on the events which took place in the evening.

Events	Matthew	Mark	Luke	John	Time
Preparation for the Passover meal	26:17-20	14:12-17	22:7-14		AM

John does not provide detail of these events. We have already
seen that John makes little mention of the intervening days
between the triumphal entry five days before the Passover
and the meal in Bethany two days before the Passover.
After talking about the triumphal entry and the time Jesus
was in the temple, John moves straight to the end of the
week. Leaving aside any mention of the preparation for the
Passover meal, he takes us straight to the meal itself.

Matthew, Mark and Luke indicate that the question, "Where
wilt thou that we prepare for thee to eat the Passover?"

came from the disciples on their own initiative (Mt. 26:17; Mk. 14:12; Lk. 22:9). This may be an indication of how Jesus was concerned for his followers to think for themselves. It would have been easy for the disciples to wait for Jesus to make the decision on everything. But Jesus, knowing that the Passover was drawing very near, waited for the disciples to take the initiative for themselves. The lesson is clear for us today. We might be inclined to leave decisions to others we think are more capable of dealing with the issues; but the lesson is that we should rely on our own initiative when we know something needs to be done, rather than waiting for others to decide.

All three records demonstrate an air of secrecy about the place where the meal was to be prepared. Doubtless all the disciples heard the instructions given to Peter and John; but the instructions, in themselves, were not sufficient for any of the disciples to know the location. Peter and John, when they entered the city, were provided with signs which Jesus had told them they would encounter. So they must have been the only two of the disciples who knew, before the meal, where it was to be held.

We know that Judas had already agreed to betray Jesus. The secrecy of the location for the Last Supper could well have been designed by Jesus in order that Judas would not be able to interfere with the meal, which was of supreme importance to Jesus. So, by organising the meal in a secret location, Jesus was planning the way in which he would be taken by the chief priests. Even in this matter his concern was for the welfare of his disciples.

Once they were in the upper room, Jesus "sat down with the twelve" (Lk. 22:14), and told his disciples, "With desire

I have desired to eat this Passover before I suffer" (22:15), and instructed the disciples about the bread and the cup. We will return to that aspect of the meal later; but it was during the meal that Jesus told his disciples: "One of you will betray me" (Mt. 26:21; Mk. 14:18; Lk. 22:31; Jno. 13:21). This announcement produced a seemingly strange response from the disciples "And there was also a strife among them, which of them should be accounted the greatest" (Lk. 22:24). It was this event which prompted Jesus to wash the disciples' feet (Jno. 13:1-20).

What shall we have therefore?

The strife about which of them should be accounted the greatest is a feature of the disciples' thought patterns right through the ministry of Jesus. In Mark 9:34 the disciples had been arguing "in the way" about this very thing. On the way to Jerusalem the same issue raised its ugly head again, when Peter asked: "What shall we have … ?" (Mt. 19:27) because the disciples had "left all" (Mk. 10:28). Jesus promised all of them that "ye which have followed me … shall sit upon twelve thrones, judging the twelve tribes of Israel" (Mt. 19:28). This promise prompted the "mother of Zebedee's children" (20:20), probably encouraged by her two sons James and John, [2] to ask that the two most important thrones of judgment be reserved for them. "And when the ten heard it, they began to be much displeased with James and John" – and well they might!

It could seem strange that the disciples responded like this in the upper room. But we need to remember that the disciples

---

2   Although it is the mother who makes the request, it is the two brothers to whom Jesus addresses his answer, as can be seen in Matthew 20:21-23, where 'she' asked, but Jesus addressed 'them'.

still did not know what was going to happen to Jesus. They had no idea that he was going to be betrayed that very night and crucified the next day. The disciples were consumed with self-interest; and we ought to be able to see ourselves in the disciples in that particular circumstance. Far too often we, too, fail to respond to the needs of others because we are so wrapped up in our own plans and expectations. We can be oblivious to the needs of others, even though the words and signs – if we looked out for them – show that there is something calling for our concern.

Anointing and washing feet: another of John's themes

While the argument continued amongst the disciples, "Jesus, knowing that the Father had given all things into his hands, and that he was come from God, and went to God; He riseth from supper, and laid aside his garments; and took a towel, and girded himself. After that he poureth water into a bason, and began to wash the disciples' feet, and to wipe them with the towel wherewith he was girded" (Jno. 13:2-6). The record could simply have told us that Jesus washed the disciples' feet; but instead, it makes extensive comment about the way in which Jesus prepared himself, and how carefully and deliberately he washed the disciples' feet.

We remember that it was John alone who recorded that, at the meal in Bethany, the feet of Jesus were anointed. And now it is John who alone describes the washing of the disciples' feet in the upper room. John, by the Spirit, clearly wants us to see the parallels between the two events. When considering the reaction of individuals at the anointing of Jesus at Bethany and the washing of the disciples' feet in the upper room some interesting features are seen.

Bethany	Upper Room
Anointing of Jesus' feet	Washing the disciples' feet
John 12:3 – feet anointed	John 13:5 – feet washed
John 12:4 – Judas indignant	John 13:8 – Peter indignant
Matthew 26:10 – Judas rebuked	John 13:10 – Peter rebuked
Matthew 26:16 – Judas seeks opportunity to betray Jesus	John 13:9 – Peter contrite

These details invite us to compare and contrast Judas and Peter. Both Judas and Peter are indignant – Judas at the 'waste' of the ointment, and Peter at the thought that Jesus might wash his feet. Both were reproved by Jesus. Judas was invited to consider that the poor were always with them. Peter needed to understand that he had to learn humility and to accept the consequences of his unwillingness to be the servant. Judas did not learn the lesson, whilst Peter was of a totally different make-up. Peter was willing to accept the Lord's rebuke; and this marks the difference between the two. They both figure prominently in the last two meals that Jesus shared, and both miss the point of what is happening. Judas could not respond to the Lord. But Peter did.

Judas demonstrated that he was not at one with Jesus and the disciples during both the meal in Bethany and the meal in the upper room. Judas left the meal in Bethany to go and arrange the betrayal with the chief priest (Mk. 14:10); and although the records are not explicit, this must have been at night, as the meal will have taken place during the evening. Judas also left the upper room to go to the chief priests, "and it was night" (Jno. 13:30). On these two occasions, during intimate meals, Judas showed that his mind was elsewhere. He was more concerned to receive the "reward of iniquity" (Acts 1:18) than to have fellowship with his Lord and the other disciples.

Consecration for the work

Before moving on to consider the disciples' question ('Is it I?'), there is another aspect of the washing of the disciples' feet that is worth noting.

Whilst it appears that the question was prompted by the disciples arguing about who was to be the greatest (Lk. 22:24), it seems to me that there was also something else going on; namely that Jesus, by this washing, was consecrating his disciples for the work they were to carry out after his ascension. This is suggested by a number of similarities between the language of John and the consecration of Aaron and his sons in Leviticus.

John	Language	Leviticus
13:3	all into his hands	8:27
13:4	laid aside garments	6:11
13:4	girded himself	8:7
13:5	water wash	8:6
13:9	feet hands head	8:23
13:10	washed	8:6

Peter's request that Jesus should wash his head, hands and feet perhaps indicates that John wants his readers to understand that Peter, eventually, saw the significance of what Jesus was doing. And to this we may also add the three times (John 17:6,9,11) that Jesus, in prayer, gives thanks to his Father for the disciples whom God had given him.

The exhortation for us is clear:

- The Levites were separated for service by birth;

- The disciples were ceremonially separated to the Lord's service by the washing of their feet;

- We are separated for service by our birth into Christ at baptism.

Is it I?

The reaction of the disciples to the Lord's comment, "One of you will betray me" (Mt. 26:21), is worthy of note. The majority of the disciples say: "*Lord*, is it I?" (26:22); but Judas says: "*Master*, is it I?" (26:25). Now whilst Jesus was both 'Lord' and 'Master' to the disciples, the difference is most significant. The disciples regarded Jesus as their 'Lord'. He was the one to be observed unfailingly. But Judas looked on Jesus only as his "Master" – that is to say, *Rabbi*. To Judas, Jesus was simply another teacher – a man who, while having useful things to say, was not the only authority. Jesus catches these two aspects of the disciples' response by saying, when he washed their feet in response to their arguing about who would be greatest, "Ye call me Master and Lord: and ye say well; for so I am" (Jno. 13:13), highlighting that not only was he their 'Master' – their *Rabbi* – but he was also their 'Lord', by which he put his teaching above question. Judas seems to have failed to see this distinction. His response to the call of Jesus, then, may well have just been an intellectual acknowledgement of the message. We must recognise the emotional impact of the message also. Jesus is not only a teacher, but he is also one who demands total loyalty.

The same night in which he was betrayed …

When Paul introduces the breaking of bread in 1 Corinthians 11, he reminds us of Judas' behaviour when he writes, "For I have received of the Lord that which also I delivered unto you, That the Lord Jesus the same *night in which he was betrayed took bread*" (1 Cor. 11:23). This is a clear reference to the betrayal of the Lord by Judas Iscariot. Our familiarity with the record probably means that we do not notice that this is a rather discordant way to introduce the breaking of bread. The reason for this is because there was a discordant spirit in the ecclesia at Corinth, just as there was in the upper room. So the Apostle is concerned to focus the believer's mind on the possibility of going through the ritual of the breaking of bread without having a mind which has been affected by what it actually entailed for Jesus.

We have already seen that Judas had planned to absent himself from the meal in the upper room in order to conclude his evil deal with the chief priests. The night before, he had made the arrangement to deliver Jesus to them (Mt. 26:14-15). Now he was looking for an opportunity. That evening, when the disciples and Jesus were on their own, would be the ideal time. Doubtless that was why Jesus kept the location of the meal secret from the majority of the disciples. Now that Judas knew where they would be, he would be able to advise the chief priests, and they would be able to come and capture him without the knowledge of the common people. All through the meal Judas would be seeking an opportunity to leave and to make his way to the chief priests. His mind would not be on the matters taking place in the upper room. He had another agenda.

This matches the mental state of some of those in the ecclesia in Corinth, as Paul said: "When ye come together therefore into one place, this is not to eat the Lord's supper" (1 Cor. 11:20). Some were viewing the memorial service as an opportunity to have a good meal and to get drunk. Others came hungry and were not satisfied. Some, like Judas, had a different agenda, with their minds on other things. Consequently, the real purpose of their meeting together was lost on them. There was, therefore, in Corinth, a great need for self-examination. Each brother and sister needed to examine their own motives and thoughts when they came together to eat the "Lord's supper". It is for this reason that Paul concludes his argument: "But let a man examine himself, and so let him eat of that bread, and drink of that cup" (11:28). They needed to review their own hearts and to decide whether they were at the Lord's supper to gratify their own fleshly desires, or to remember the Lord's death and all that it signified.

In just the same way, we too must be sure of our own motives when we attend the memorial service. We must make sure that we do not have a hidden agenda, with our minds elsewhere.

Questions, questions …

What follows in John's record is a series of questions by various of the disciples which show that they still did not understand the significance of what Jesus was saying. Jesus still had much to tell them and only a short time to say it. Yet he never cuts the disciples' questions short; nor does he ignore their questions in order to tell them the things that are on his mind. He always leaves the particular point he is making to deal with the disciples' questions before continuing with his instructions.

First, however, it is worth reflecting on the way in which Jesus handled the questions. He knew that later that night he would be betrayed by Judas and that the next day he would be crucified. Against that background, with a great deal of information that he still wanted to impart to the disciples within a short time frame, he continued with his customary calm and thoroughness. Here was a man who, despite knowing that his time had come (Jno. 13:1), demonstrated true patience and self-control. His primary focus was to resolve the disciples' problems. The fact that he had already explained things to them without them understanding in no way affected how Jesus spoke to them. If only we could be so patient with our brethren and sisters! We never work under the kind of strain under which our Lord laboured that evening; and yet we do not manifest the concern that our Lord showed at that time. There is a clear lesson to be learned here from the patience of Jesus in such a pressurised situation.

And so we come on to the disciples' questions:

Scripture	Disciple	Question
John 13:36	Peter	"Whither goest thou?"
John 13:37	Peter	"Why cannot I follow thee now?"
John 14:5	Thomas	"How can we know the way?"
John 14:8	Philip	"Shew us the Father"
John 14:22	Judas (not Iscariot)	"How wilt thou manifest thyself to us and not unto the world?"

The disciples' questions, their interrelation, and the degree to which the disciples understood Jesus' answers, provide the basis for the rest of the things that Jesus says to the disciples in the upper room and on the way down to the Kidron. Unless we can understand the questions, we will not gain the greatest benefit from these chapters in John's Gospel. A clear understanding of John 14-17 hinges on a proper appreciation of the questions that the disciples asked.

Peter

Peter asks two related questions: "Whither goest thou?" (Jno. 13:36), and "Why cannot I follow thee now?" (13:37). Peter – and the others for that matter – had been with Jesus for three and a half years. They had gone everywhere with him. In fact, this was to be a condition required for the replacement for Judas in Acts 1:21 ("Wherefore of these men which have companied with us all the time that the Lord Jesus went in and out among us"). So, Peter's questions may seem surprising: they stemmed from worldly thinking, which was "from beneath" to use Jesus' earlier language. Peter was thinking of location in a *physical* sense, whereas Jesus seems to have been thinking in *spiritual* terms, in thoughts which were "from above".

Whither I go: what had Jesus said already?

The phrase "Whither I go" had occurred earlier, in Jesus' discussion with the Pharisees after the incident of the woman taken in adultery (Jno. 8:1-11). Having dismissed the woman ("Neither do I condemn thee; go, and sin no more" – 8:11), Jesus turned his attention to the woman's accusers and told them, "I am the light of the world: he that followeth me shall not walk in darkness, but shall have the light of life" (8:12). But his enemies immediately accused Jesus of not bearing true witness (8:13), to which Jesus responded: "Though I bear record of myself, yet my record is true: for

I know whence I came, and *whither I go*; but ye cannot tell whence I come, and *whither I go*" (8:14). It seems likely, on that occasion, also, that Jesus was not speaking in terms of *physical* location. The reason given as to why they were unable to tell where Jesus was going was that they judged "after the flesh" (8:15). They could not tell where Jesus came from, or where he was going, for the same reason that he had already explained to Nicodemus, to whom Jesus had said: "The wind bloweth where it listeth, and thou hearest the sound thereof, but *canst not tell whence it cometh, and whither it goeth*: so is every one that is born of the Spirit" (3:8). [3]

It seems clear from Jesus' teaching, therefore, that it is necessary to be 'born of the Spirit' to understand the things that he was saying. So, in continuing his discussion with the Pharisees in John 8, Jesus tells them: "Ye are from beneath; I am from above: ye are of this world; I am not of this world" (8:23). They had already demonstrated that they were thinking naturally, rather than spiritually, when they said, "Will he kill himself? Because he saith, *Whither I go*, ye cannot come" (8:22). So, in speaking to the disciples in the upper room, Jesus says: "Little children, yet a little while I am with you. Ye shall seek me: and *as I said unto the Jews, Whither I go*, ye cannot come; so now I say to you" (13:33). Peter, therefore, was thinking "from beneath", like "the Jews" before him. He and the rest of the disciples stood no chance of understanding Jesus: their thinking was carnal. They were not thinking in spiritual terms. And that was why Jesus could tell them: "And whither I go ye know,

---

3 A complete list of the occasions when Jesus is recorded as saying, "Whither I go, ye cannot come", is as follows: John 8:14,21,(22); 13:33,36; 14:4.

and the way ye know" (14:4). They had been with Jesus
for over three years. They had seen the miracles and heard
his teaching: they knew it, but they did not, as yet, fully
understand it. They could not lift their thoughts above
the natural. Because Peter did not understand that Jesus
was speaking of things "from above", he was unable to
understand why he was not able to 'go' with Jesus.

In this the disciples are so like us. So often we spend our
time and effort talking about and debating trivial issues. We
fail to appreciate the magnitude of the Father's provision,
and we debate things of little consequence, not seeing the
beauty of the spiritual things to which we are called.

Thomas

By this point in the conversation (in John 14), Thomas is
deeply perplexed. Despite the fact that Jesus has previously
spoken of 'going', Thomas declares: "Whither thou goest
we know not, and how can we know the way?" (14:5). Like
Peter, Thomas is thinking 'from beneath'; and so Jesus gives
Thomas a response similar to that which he has already
given to Peter. He says: "I am the way, the truth, and the
life: no man cometh unto the Father, but by me" (14:6). The
Lord's response is worth breaking down into its constituent
elements: 'the way', 'the truth', and 'the life'.

- *The way* – Jesus had already taught the disciples, "All
  things are delivered unto me of my Father: and no man
  knoweth the Son, but the Father; neither knoweth any
  man the Father, save the Son, and he to whomsoever
  the Son will reveal him" (Mt. 11:27). The way to God
  was (and remains) through an understanding of the
  work of Jesus. On a later occasion, Jesus was even

more specific, in saying: "I am the door: by me if any man enter in, he shall be saved, and shall go in and out, and find pasture" (Jno. 10:9).

- *The truth* – It was later written of Jesus that "the Word was made flesh, and dwelt among us, (and we beheld his glory, the glory as of the only begotten of the Father,) full of grace and *truth*" (1:14). But Jesus had taught the Pharisees who, as we have seen earlier, were thinking 'from beneath', that if they came to "know *the truth*", then it would "make (them) free" (8:32). In that same conversation, Jesus also challenged them about the truth of what he was saying: "... if I say the truth, why do ye not believe me?" (8:46).

- *The life* – In the prologue to his Gospel, John wrote about Jesus that "in him was life; and the life was the light of men" (1:4). And even though this was written *after* Thomas's question in the upper room, the principles bound up in John's words were contained in the teaching of Jesus that Thomas will have heard, as recorded in John 14:6. After the healing of the impotent man on the Sabbath (5:9), Jesus, confronted by "the Jews", taught them that he was able to raise the dead and bring anyone to life: "For as the Father raiseth up the dead, and quickeneth them; even so the Son quickeneth whom he will" (5:21). The person 'quickened' is the one who hears and believes the word of Jesus: "Verily, verily, I say unto you, He that heareth my word, and believeth on Him that sent me, hath everlasting life, and shall not come into condemnation; but is passed from death unto life" (5:24). This link between hearing the word of Jesus and obeying his teaching is reinforced later when, disputing with the Pharisees, Jesus tells them: "Verily, verily, I say unto you, If a man keep my saying, he shall never see death" (8:51).

When Jesus spoke of being the "door of the sheep", he continued by teaching the disciples that 'the way' through this 'door' led to life: "I give unto them eternal life; and they shall never perish, neither shall any man pluck them out of my hand" (10:28). Peter had appreciated these points earlier, too, for when he was asked by Jesus whether he and the other disciples would forsake him as the crowds had done, Peter responded: "Lord, to whom shall we go? thou hast the words of eternal life" (6:68).

How often, then, do we fail to appreciate that Jesus is 'the way'? Why do we prefer so often to work out our own 'way' of doing things? It is not naïve of us to ask, 'What would Jesus do in this situation?' – such a question would undoubtedly help us to establish and follow the way which leads to life (Mt. 7:14).

Philip

Jesus' final words to Thomas ("If ye had known me, ye should have known my Father also: and from henceforth ye know Him, and have seen Him" – John 14:7) prompted from Philip the seemingly simple request: "Lord, shew us the Father, and it sufficeth us" (14:8). But this request from Philip showed the same lack of comprehension seen in both Peter and Thomas.

Only a few days earlier, Jesus had said, "And he that seeth me seeth Him that sent me" (12:45). And this statement was in itself simply a summary of things that Jesus had taught during his ministry. The works Jesus performed demonstrated that the Father was "in" Jesus, and that Jesus was "in" the Father (10:38). Or again, Jesus had said: "The Son can do nothing of himself, but what he seeth the Father do: for what things soever He (the Father) doeth, these also doeth the Son likewise" (5:19). It was possible to 'see" God in Jesus because he did the works of the Father, and Jesus' doctrine was not his, "but His that sent (him)" (7:16).

Having told Philip that he was a manifestation of the Father, Jesus went on to talk to Philip about how things would be after Jesus has been taken from them by the crucifixion. Jesus was no ordinary preacher or prophet: his teaching to the disciples (which Philip had not understood) was that Jesus had been sent by God. He had come "in the name of the father" (Mt. 28:19); therefore Philip and the rest of the disciples had 'seen" the Father already, though they did not appreciate that fact.

How often do we see Jesus' teaching as an 'inconvenient' set of truths? His words place constraints upon our lives – constraints which are actually designed to make us less like Adam and more like the Father. And, if only we can accept these inconveniences, the teaching of Jesus provides us with an opportunity to 'show the Father' to those around us.

Philip and the Comforter

Jesus' promise of the Comforter must be seen in the context in which the promise is made. Whilst the promise had a more general application than simply to Philip, it was made in the first place to Philip against the background of his own confusion. If we understand that situation and what Jesus was telling Philip, we should be able to gain a clear understanding of Bible teaching about the Comforter.

Having told Philip that "he that hath seen me hath seen the Father" (Jno. 14:9), Jesus develops the implications of this important statement. First, Jesus goes on to explain to Philip: "Verily, verily, I say unto you, He that believeth on me, the works that I do shall he do also; and greater works than these shall he do; because I go unto my Father" (14:12). There are two parts to this promise:

1. *For Philip* – if he believes, then he and the disciples will do 'the works' of Jesus;

2. *For Philip and the disciples* – they would do even 'greater' works.

These promises would be fulfilled after Jesus had ascended to heaven. But how would they be fulfilled in the lives of the disciples?

The disciples had been sent out "to preach the kingdom of God, and to heal the sick" (Lk. 9:2); and "when they were returned, [they] told him all that they had done" (9:10). So it appears that they had already done at least some of 'the works' that Jesus had done. Jesus was therefore telling Philip and the other disciples that after he had been taken from them they would continue to perform miraculous works, such as healing the sick, as well as preaching the Kingdom of God. But what about the 'greater works'?

After the resurrection of Jesus, Peter and John are recorded as performing miracles and preaching the Kingdom of God. The response to their work was phenomenal. On one occasion, 3,000 were baptised (Acts 2:41), and another time 5,000 believed (4:4). In bringing the preaching of Jesus to fruition, such early responses to the preaching of the apostles seem to have been greater than the responses Jesus himself had during his earthly ministry. So perhaps these were the "greater works".

We will return in due course to the matter of 'keeping the commandments', which Jesus raises in this conversation with Philip.

Judas (not Iscariot)

Judas then takes his turn at questioning Jesus. His puzzlement is that Jesus will manifest himself to them but not to 'the world'. Judas was clearly thinking in visible, tangible terms; but Jesus was trying to help him understand the more subtle, spiritual sense in which Jesus would "come and make (his) abode" with the disciples (Jno. 14:23). This kind of fellowship with the disciples (including Thomas) was something that 'the world' could not experience or understand.

When John the Baptist introduced Jesus as the Lamb of God (1:36), two of John's disciples followed Jesus. The conversation which resulted ended with those two disciples going to see where Jesus dwelt. The record says that they "*abode* with him that day" (1:39). Later, using the same word, Jesus said: "He that eateth my flesh, and drinketh my blood, *dwelleth* in me, and I in him" (6:56). This 'dwelling' is also associated with *keeping* God's word; for, speaking to the Jewish leaders who were beginning to believe in him, Jesus said: "If ye *continue* [same word as 'abide', 'dwell'] in my word, then are ye my disciples indeed" (8:31).

Abiding in mansions

It was Peter's questions that prompted Jesus' discourse about "many mansions" (14:1). The chapter division is most unhelpful. Jesus' final comment to Peter ("And whither

I go ye know, and the way ye know" – 14:4) prompted Thomas to ask his question. In speaking to Peter, also, about the "many _mansions_" in his Father's house, Jesus used a word very closely related to the word for 'abide', 'dwell', 'continue' that he used in answering Judas' query. In using this particular language, Jesus was picking up again the theme of 'abiding' that starts in John 1 and is developed in John 6 and 8. Jesus is reminding Peter of the work that will be achieved by his death and resurrection. Peter is being taught that the temporary dwelling/abiding with Jesus will be transformed into a permanent dwelling by the resurrection that Peter himself will eventually experience.

The number of times that Jesus uses the word 'abide' in the upper room and on the way to the Garden of Gethsemane should cause us to ponder on his teaching to the disciples. The lesson for us is clear: continuing ('abiding') in Jesus' words, and making his life our own, will assure us of a permanent 'abiding place' in the Kingdom of God when Jesus returns.

A major theme

The list of occurrences in John 14 and 15 (below) of the Greek word translated 'mansions' in the Authorised Version, and the related words for 'abide', 'dwell', 'continue' and 'remain', reveals what a major theme this represents both in the upper room and on the way towards the Garden of Gethsemane.

The use of monai / meno ('mansions'/'abide') on the last night of Jesus' mortal life

- _14:2_ – 'mansions'
- _14:23_ – 'abode'

- *14:10* – 'dwelleth'
- *14:16* – 'abide'
- *14:17* – 'dwelleth'
- *14:25* – 'present'
- *15:4* – 'abide' (×3)
- *15:5* – 'abideth'
- *15:6* – 'abide'
- *15:7* – 'abide' (×2)
- *15:9* – 'continue'
- *15:10* – 'abide' (×2)
- *15:11* – 'remain'
- *15:16* – 'remain'

The emphasis Jesus put on this theme of 'abiding' was a key part of the Lord's compassionate response to Peter in his need to be reassured after being told that he would shortly deny Jesus (13:38). The explanation to Peter, and the rest of the disciples, was that Jesus' death and resurrection was an essential part of the plan that the Father had set in motion so that Jesus and his disciples could be together for ever (14:3). The 'abiding' of Jesus is designed to match the way that the Father *abides* in Jesus (14:10). This *abiding* of the Father was the means whereby Jesus was able to perform his 'works' (14:10); and the evidence that Jesus and the Father were *abiding* in the believers would be the works that they too would be able to do (14:12-14). The way that this *abiding* would be achieved would be seen by Jesus and his Father *both* coming and making their abode with the disciples (14:23). Jesus was speaking of the fellowship that would exist between the believer, the Father and their saviour, the risen Lord. [4]

Departure from the upper room

"Arise, let us go hence" (14:31) marks the departure from the upper room. But the theme of 'abiding' continues during the walk towards the Brook Kidron, which is not encountered until John 18:1.

Jesus now begins an expanded explanation as to how the disciples are to *abide* in him and also why they must continue to allow him to *abide* in them. What follows is crucial for us today. Whilst we do not have the power of the Holy Spirit to work miracles, it is important for us to appreciate our need to allow Jesus and the Father to "come ... and make (their) abode with (us)" (14:23).

Abiding in the vine

By developing the parable of the vine in John 15, Jesus shows the importance of the *abiding* of the Father and the Son in the believer.

Israel were a "noble vine" (Jer. 2:21); but because they did not abide in the commandment, they became "degenerate" (2:21). Likewise, the believer today who does not 'abide' in Jesus (Jno. 15:4, 5, 6, 7) will not bear fruit (Jno. 15:4-7), and will consequently, like an unfruitful vine, be "taken away" (15:2). Both the first-century believers and we ourselves have been given the warning from the example of Israel: "God

---

4   It is important to notice the emphasis on the promised fellowship in John 14:23 ("If a man love me ... we will come ... and make our abode with him"). This contrasts sharply with the erroneous view that Jesus enters our heart at baptism.

spared not the natural branches" of the olive tree "because of unbelief" (Rom. 11:20-21). We must therefore take heed.

As Jesus explains, the way for the believer to bring forth fruit is to "keep (the Lord's) commandments" (Jno. 15:10); for in so doing believers will "abide in (his) love" (15:10). In unfolding this teaching to his disciples, Jesus was creating an environment which, after his departure, they might be better able to remember, so that in keeping his commandments, his "joy might remain" in them.

Developing Old Testament teaching

It turns out, too, that Jesus, in speaking to his disciples about 'abiding', was developing the earlier teaching of the Old Testament about the Father's wish to 'dwell' with men. God told Moses:

- *Exodus 25:8* – "And let them make Me a sanctuary; that I may dwell among them"; and again:
- *Exodus 29:45-46* – "And I will dwell among the children of Israel, and will be their God. And they shall know that I am the LORD their God, that brought them forth out of the land of Egypt, that I may dwell among them: I am the LORD their God".

So we see that God had a plan which involved Him being with His people.

When David had a desire to build a house for God, he was reminded that God had walked with His people through the wilderness (2 Sam. 7:5-7), and that whilst David was not to build an house for God, a house would be built for David (7:27). This was an extension of the teaching in Exodus that God wished to dwell with men. The promise that David would have a house built for him showed that God's 'dwelling' was to be in people, which is something that David clearly understood when he wrote:

"Except the LORD build the house, they labour in vain that build it: except the LORD keep the city, the watchman waketh but in vain. It is vain for you to rise up early, to sit up late, to eat the bread of sorrows: for so He giveth His beloved sleep. Lo, children are an heritage of the LORD: and the fruit of the womb is His reward" (Ps. 127:1-3).

Part of the divine plan

The birth of a saviour had been long promised: "Therefore the LORD Himself shall give you a sign; Behold, a virgin shall conceive, and bear a son, and shall call his name Immanuel" (Isa. 7:14). And Matthew confirms for us in no uncertain terms the meaning of the name Immanuel: "Behold, a virgin shall be with child, and shall bring forth a son, and they shall call his name Emmanuel, which being interpreted is, God with us" (Mt. 1:23). Yet again, therefore, it is made clear that the Father had always planned to "abide" with His people. And the mechanism by which God's 'abiding' was to be achieved could now be seen to be the raising up of His own Son – the son of David and the seed of the woman. Through his death and resurrection Jesus was to be the "firstborn" (Col. 1:15) of a new creation, which was to be the "temple of the living God" (2 Cor. 6:16).

In fact, Jesus had already hinted at this plan very early on in his ministry, recorded significantly in John's Gospel, when he said: "Destroy this temple, and in three days I will raise it up. Then said the Jews, Forty and six years was this temple in building, and wilt thou rear it up in three days? But he spake of *the temple of his body*" (Jno. 2:19-21).

The saving work of Jesus

Peter was not able to 'go' with Jesus (13:36) because Jesus was going to do something by his going away which only he could do. That is, to obtain "eternal salvation" through his death and resurrection (Heb. 5:9). Peter clearly did not understand this; if he had understood, Peter would never have rashly said to Jesus, "I will lay down my life for thy sake" (Jno. 13:37). His allegiance to his Lord was never in question. Jesus knew what was in Peter's heart (2:25) and did not even need to hear any words from him. Peter's mistake was in offering to do what his Lord was about to do. Whereas the Lord was sinless, Peter clearly was not; he did not yet understand the redemptive work of Jesus, nor his own need for a sinless man to die on his behalf. The rebuke of the Lord, therefore, was absolutely essential: "The cock shall not crow, till thou hast denied me thrice" (13:38). Peter had to understand his own weakness in contrast with the confidence of the Master in the Father.

Thomas at least acknowledged his lack of understanding when he said, "We know not whither thou goest; and how can we know the way?" (14:5). And yet he had been given many opportunities to "know the way" and to understand the saving work that Jesus would perform. Looking back in later years, the Apostle John remembered and recorded some of the many pointers that Jesus had given them all in the weeks and months before his death:

- *John 6:35* – "And Jesus said unto them, I am the bread of life: *he that cometh to me* shall never hunger; and he that believeth on me shall never thirst".

- *John 6:51* – "I am the living bread which came down from heaven: *if any man eat of this bread, he shall live forever*: and the bread that I will give is my flesh, which I will give for the life of the world".

- *John 8:12* – "Then spake Jesus again unto them, saying, I am the light of the world: *he that followeth me shall not walk in darkness*, but shall have the light of life".

- *John 10:9* – "I am the door: by me *if any man enter in, he shall be saved*, and shall go in and out, and find pasture".

- *John 10:11* – "I am the good shepherd: *the good shepherd giveth his life* for the sheep".

- *John 11:25* – "Jesus said unto her, I am the resurrection, and the life: *he that believeth in me, though he were dead, yet shall he live*".

- *John 14:6* – "Jesus saith unto him, I am the way, the truth, and the life: *no man cometh unto the Father, but by me*".

The words in *italic* type in these passages from John provide a composite picture of what Thomas, and the other disciples, had already been told about the role that Jesus would play in their salvation. Piecing these key points together produces a very comprehensive overview of the Lord's saving work. Of course, Jesus had said even more than this, telling them plainly that he was to be crucified and would rise again (Mt. 16:21; 17:23; 20:19; Mk. 9:31; 10:34; Lk. 9:22; 18:33). Yet the disciples did not even understand such plain speaking, because they were "slow of heart to believe" (Lk. 24:25) what they had heard Jesus say. The disciples – and Thomas in particular at this point – did not comprehend what they had been told, even though they *knew* what they had heard. It is important to appreciate that Jesus expected them to accept what he had said. Thomas needed to appreciate that the way to fellowship with the Father and the Son – their 'abiding' – was only through Jesus (14:6); and that this was going to be effected only by Jesus going away first.

And, lest we attempt to excuse our own slowness in understanding and, consequently, believing all that we read in Scripture, we do well to remember that Jesus "upbraided them with their unbelief" (Mk. 16:14). Would we not be reproved by the Lord for our not infrequent incomprehension of the word of God? For example, how firmly do we believe this divine assurance: "I will never leave thee nor forsake thee" – a promise made quite often to the faithful (Deut. 31:6; Josh. 1:5; 1 Chron. 28:20; Isa. 41:13; Heb. 13:5)? How closely do we associate ourselves with the related promise: "We will come and make our abode with (you)" (Jno. 14:23)?

Showing the Father

Jesus concludes his response to Thomas with the words, "From henceforth ye have seen the Father" (14:7); and it is this remark that causes the perplexed Philip to ask, "Show us the Father" (14:8). And Philip's request highlights another, related, gap in the disciples' understanding. Philip, and probably the others also, had failed to grasp that Jesus 'declared' the Father (1:18). Whilst Jesus told Philip that "he that hath seen me hath seen the Father" (14:9), the Lord was not inviting Philip (or anyone else) to focus on *physical* appearance. Philip would know well the Old Testament teaching that "no man can see Me and live" (Ex. 33:20). Schooled in the Jewish way of thinking, Philip would surely appreciate that when Moses asked to see God, he was 'shown' the divine qualities and characteristics of the LORD (Ex. 33:18-20).

But Judas (not Iscariot) is still perplexed. He wants to know how Jesus will manifest himself to the disciples but not to the world (Jno. 14:22). He was clearly locked into the idea of seeing the physical Jesus. Jesus, in his explanation to Judas, continues to develop the concept of the 'abiding' of the Father and the Son with the believer. Jesus was to be *manifest in the disciples* to the extent that they 'kept' his words: "If a man love me, he will keep my words: and my Father will love him, and we will come unto him, and make our abode with him" (14:23). This teaching was presented by Jesus when he was with them; but the Comforter would come and "teach them all things" (14:26). These words were intended as a source of reassurance to all the disciples in the context of Jesus' teaching about his 'manifestation' of the Father's character and of their joint 'abiding' with those who were faithful.

Still in the upper room at this point, Jesus repeats the calming words from his conversation with Peter (14:1): "Let not your heart be troubled" (14:27). And, having come only so far in the education of his disciples, Jesus and the eleven sing a hymn (Mt. 26:30) then leave the upper room. John marks this departure with the words of Jesus "Arise, let us go hence" (Jno. 14:31).

Keeping the commandment

All the questions from the disciples had been raised after Jesus had said, "A new commandment I give unto you, That ye love one another; as I have loved you" (13:34).

Jesus now returns to this theme as they leave the upper room. This was, in a sense, the essence of Jesus' teaching; and it was not lost on the Apostle John who, in later years, underlined the link between the Lord's commandment to love one's fellow man and loving God Himself: "If a man say, I love God, and hateth his brother, he is a liar: for he that loveth not his brother whom he hath seen, how can he love God whom he hath not seen?" (1 Jno. 4:20). The keeping of the commandment means that the believer will be like Jesus – he will be *Christlike*. In this way, the believer will manifest God to those who see him. So just as Jesus could say, "He that hath seen me hath seen the Father" (14:49), Jesus expects that those who see us will see at least something of the Father also.

The Lord's promised 'coming' and the promise of the Comforter[5]

We must read the record carefully if we are to understand correctly what Jesus promised his disciples about the effects of his going away. There were two different promises, and they are considered in turn below.

1. I/we will come:

- *John 14:3* – "And if I go and prepare a place for you, *I will come again*, and receive you unto myself; that where I am, there ye may be also".

- *John 14:18* – "I will not leave you comfortless (Gk. *orphanous* – 'as orphans'): *I will come to you*".

---

5 A more comprehensive review of this topic can be found in *'Spirit' in the New Testament*, by Edward Whittaker and Reg Carr (Norwich: The Testimony, 1985).

- *John 14:23* – "Jesus answered and said unto him, If a man love me, he will keep my words: and my Father will love him, and <u>we will come unto him</u>, and make our abode with him".

- *John 14:28* – "Ye have heard how I said unto you, <u>I</u> go away, and <u>come again unto you</u>. If ye loved me, ye would rejoice, because I said, I go unto the Father: for my Father is greater than I".

This first group of passages focuses on the fact that, even though Jesus was going to be taken away from the disciples, his glorified state would enable him to continue to be 'with' his disciples. His eternal nature would enable him to fellowship his believers, right throughout the ages.

Nor is there any difficulty in understanding the concept of God being 'with' His servants, even though He is not physically present with them. Consider the following passages:

1. *Genesis 39:2* – "And the LORD was with Joseph".

2. *Joshua 6:27* – "So the LORD was with Joshua".

3. *Judges 2:18* – "And when the LORD raised them up judges, then the LORD was with the judge".

4. *1 Samuel 18:14* – "And David behaved himself wisely in all his ways; and the LORD was with him".

5. *1 Chronicles 9:20* – "And Phinehas the son of Eleazar was the ruler over them in time past, and the LORD was with him".

Passages 1, 2, 4, and 5 show that Yahweh can be 'with' a man, whilst 3 shows that He can equally well be 'with' a number of individuals. God was 'with' all the people mentioned in this way. The individuals each had a relationship with Him. He was their God and they placed their trust in Him. Physical separation does not necessarily destroy a relationship. We all have friends who are not with us all the time. Yet we would never suggest that such people are only friends when we are physically present with them. The hard part for us may be to appreciate that we can have a close, personal relationship with our Father and His Son when they are not physically present with us. It is true, however, that the more real and alive our friends are to us, the easier it is for us to have a meaningful relationship with them; and such relationships are spoken of in Scripture as 'fellowship'. The fellowship we have with the Father and His Son is such that they are always with us; and the keener our appreciation of this fact is, the more likely it is that it will modify our behaviour *and* our thoughts.

Fellowship with the Father is consequent on right beliefs and right actions. That is why the Apostle Paul exhorts us: "Wherefore come out from among them, and be ye separate, saith the Lord, and touch not the unclean thing; and I will receive you" (2 Cor. 6:17). This is the basis on which God will "dwell in (us), and walk in (us); and ... will be (our) God, and (we) shall be (His) people" (6:16). This is the way in which we can share in the experience of those first-century disciples to whom Jesus promised: "We will come unto him, and make our abode with him" (Jno. 14:23). This is something which all believers throughout the ages have had the privilege of sharing. It is the mystery of God made manifest: that God wishes to 'dwell with men' – with you and me.

We are exhorted also to "Let this mind be in (us), which was also in Christ Jesus" (Phil. 2:5). Paul agonised over the brethren and sisters in Galatia "until Christ be formed in (them)" (Gal. 4:19). Complacency will not receive the reward of experiencing "Christ in (us), the hope of glory" (Col. 1:27). It is our responsibility, with God's help through His Word, to develop the mind of Christ now, while looking forward to eternal and unfettered fellowship with the Father and His Son in the age to come.

2. I will send it (Gk., *pempso auton*) **unto you:**

- *John 15:26* – "But when the Comforter is come, whom *I will send unto you* from the Father, even the Spirit of truth, which proceedeth from the Father, he shall testify of me".

- *John 16:7* – "Nevertheless I tell you the truth; It is expedient for you that I go away: for if I go not away, the Comforter will not come unto you; but if I depart, *I will send him (it) unto you*".

This second promise to the disciples – the promise of the 'Comforter' is altogether different from the first. It had a miraculous fulfilment, as is self-evident from the roster of promised activities directly associated with it and which characterised its presence:

1. *John 14:16,17* – It would *replace* the disciples' miracle-working Lord.

2. *John 14:26* – It would *teach the disciples "all things"*.

3. *John 15:26,27* – It would *bear witness* (through preaching) to the Lord.

4. *John 16:7-11* – It would convince (*i.e., 'convict'*) *the world* of sin, righteousness, and judgment.

5. *John 16:13-15* – It would guide the disciples into *all truth*.

Passages 1, 3, and 5 are interrelated. They each reflect the way in which the Comforter would continue the work that Jesus had begun with the disciples; and it would act as a guarantor that their future teaching would be consistent with what Jesus had taught them. It would "guide (them) into all truth" (16:13). It would "give (them) a mouth and wisdom, which all (their) adversaries (were not) able to gainsay nor resist" (Lk. 21:15). So they would be able to take comfort in the fact that they would be able to "take no thought how or what thing (they should) answer, or what (they might) say" (12:11) This was because of the related promise, given directly to them: "The Holy (Spirit) shall teach you in the same hour what ye ought to say" (Lk. 12:12).

That the Comforter would be with them "forever" (Jno. 14:16, AV) should not mislead us into thinking that the Comforter is promised to all believers *throughout the ages*. The Greek word *aion* does not imply eternity: its scope is qualified by the context in which it occurs. It is used to denote a limited time period (Mt. 12:32; 13:22) and is also sometimes translated "world" (as in 1 Corinthians 2:6).

The Comforter – the powerful, miracle-working gifts of the Holy Spirit – was promised to the disciples of Jesus who had been with him during his ministry. It would therefore be possible for it to "bring all things to your remembrance, whatsoever I have said unto you" (Jno. 14:26). Common logic dictates that this could only apply to those who had personally heard Jesus' teaching.

Whilst the reassuring promise to all Christ's followers, of any age in history ("We will come unto him, and make our abode with him" (14:23) can be a great comfort as a reality in our own lives, the promise of the Comforter served a very different, and time-limited, purpose. It was an additional comfort for those, and only those, who had heard Jesus speak that promise to them.

Out and down to the Kidron

Events	Matthew	Mark	Luke	John	Time
Abide in me				15	Night
I go my way				16	Night
Jesus lifted up his eyes to heaven				17	Night

We cannot be sure what time in the evening it was when Jesus and the eleven left the upper room. We can, however, make an educated guess. If we assume that the meal began at sunset (6.30pm), we might conjecture that the meal, the washing of the disciples feet, the discussions that took place and the singing of the hymn (Mt. 26:30; Mk. 14:26) took from two to three hours. Thus we can imagine that when they left the upper room it would be 9pm at the earliest. But we should not assume that they were groping round the city and across the Kidron Valley in pitch darkness, even though they did not have electric street lighting. Passover was the 14th day of the first month (Lev. 23:5), and the new moon marked the beginning of the month (Num. 10:10). The feast of Passover was held halfway through a lunar month, so there would have been a full moon when Jesus and the disciples left the upper room. We do not know exactly where the upper room was in the city; nor do we know the direction that the group took as they walked through the city and across the Kidron Valley to the Garden of Gethsemane. We cannot even be sure of the precise location of Gethsemane itself. And yet it remains possible still to form a picture of the journey and the circumstances; and this can serve to enhance our appreciation of the things that were said and done at that time.

Leaving the upper room, Jesus begins to tell the eleven: "I am the true vine" (Jno. 15:1). This was not a new topic unrelated to the previous discussion concerning 'abiding'. As we have already seen, the word 'abide' in John 15 is the same word as seen in the discussions in John 14. This suggests that Jesus was extending his 'abiding' theme as he explained the consequences of failing to manifest his love.

There is now a more urgent, warning tone as Jesus introduces the concept of the Father chastening His children so that the vine might "bring forth more fruit" (15:2). Jesus presents the chastening in terms of a husbandman tending a vine. For just as the husbandman cuts off any unfruitful, dead or dying branches so as not to diminish the vine's strength, so he carefully prunes fruitful boughs so that their potential might be maximized. In just the same way, the Father works with His sons and daughters. His pruning process has an ultimately helpful, cleansing effect. Consider, for example, these two verses:

- *John 15:2* – "Every branch in me that beareth not fruit He taketh away: and every branch that beareth fruit, He *purgeth* it, that it may bring forth more fruit".

- *John 15:3* – "Now ye are *clean* through the word which I have spoken unto you". [6]

---

6   The *italicised* words are translated from the same Greek word.

Now we know that the way for a "young man to cleanse his way is by taking heed thereto according to (God's) word" (Ps. 119:9). That passage is clearly what Jesus was drawing on in John 15:3, for he has already said, "If any man love me he will keep my words and we will come unto him and make *our abode* with him" (14:23). The converse of keeping the Lord's words is very distressing – as Jesus says: "If any man *abide* not in me he is cast forth as a branch and is withered; and men gather them, and cast them into the fire, and they are burned" (15:6). If we do 'abide' in him we will actually glorify God (15:8). To abide in him, we must bear fruit by keeping his commandments; and by so doing the Father is glorified. This was how Jesus himself manifested God to the people during his ministry. By doing the will of the Father, Jesus both retained his Father's fellowship and also pleased Him, for we read: "The Father hath not left me alone; for I do always the things which please Him" (8:29). We must ask ourselves, therefore, how we see our lives as both glorifying the Father and maintaining our fellowship with Him. This is the thrust of what Jesus, who was about to depart out of this world, was saying to his disciples.

Jesus continues by presenting to his disciples the ultimate manifestation of love: "Greater love hath no man than this, that a man lay down his life for his friends" (15:13). We notice that, though clearly speaking of his own impending death to redeem his brethren, Jesus uses (perhaps even quotes?) the earlier words of Peter ("I will lay down my life", 13:37). The impact of Jesus' use of those words would doubtless have startled Peter, and possibly the others who had heard Peter's affirmation in the upper room. Yet it is clear that this is the kind of self-sacrificial commitment required of Jesus' disciples. This was not the first time that

Jesus had spoken of giving his life for his followers – he had already spoken directly a number of times about his crucifixion. He had also forewarned them in less obvious ways, for example: "God so loved the world that He gave His only begotten son" (3:16); "I am the good shepherd: the good shepherd giveth his life for the sheep" (10:11).

Some of Jesus' disciples did in fact lay down their lives for him. A consideration of the Acts of the Apostles provides us with the names of some who did show that they were Jesus' friends in the way that they showed their commitment to him. But, of course, a willingness to give one's life for the sake of others, as Moses offered to do, would not achieve the desired end that the Father had in mind. Neither Moses (Ex. 32:32) nor Peter (Jno. 13:27) was sinless, so their willingness to die for others would not have sufficed for the redemption of mankind. We have not had to make this kind of supreme sacrifice; but we are faced with the challenge of an important, personal sacrifice. "Present your bodies a living sacrifice", says Paul, "which is your reasonable service" (Rom. 12:1).

The high calling of God in Christ

At this point in the narrative, Jesus reminds his disciples of their high calling. They had continued with him during his three-and-a-half-year ministry, but they still needed to be reminded: "Ye have not chosen me, but I have chosen you" (Jno. 15:16). The call of the Lord's earliest disciples is unique. It provides a pattern of the relationship that we have with the Father through Jesus: it is those "ordained to eternal life" (Acts 13:48), through their belief of the gospel, who are the "called of Jesus Christ" (Rom. 1:6). And just as the disciples were called that they "should go and bring forth fruit" (Jno. 15:16), so we must do likewise.

Jesus' cruel death is now close at hand and the disciples still do not understand. They must be prepared for this evil act; which is why Jesus proceeds to explain why he is hated and how that will be reflected in their lives too (15:17-19). The disciples were to experience first-hand this hatred not many days afterwards, when they began to preach the risen Christ. They anticipated that hatred at the time of Jesus' death and when he was in the tomb, for they all "forsook him and fled" (Mt. 26:56; Mk. 14:50); and when he was in the tomb, they were in hiding "for fear of the Jews" (Jno. 20:19).

Jesus reminds his disciples also that "the servant is not greater than his lord" (15:20), and that they, as servants, will have to suffer the same things as their Master. If they were to reflect on what they had seen during the last three-and-a-half years, they would understand what was in store for them. There had been more who persecuted Jesus and relatively few who loved him. Those who loved him could easily be identified. They kept Jesus' sayings, and would continue to keep them (15:20).

Jesus warned them, too, that they should avoid those who did not do the works of the Father, for those who hated him also hated the Father (15:23). It seems clear, at least, from the record in Acts, that the disciples did try to avoid those who hated the Father. But we need to ask ourselves, perhaps more than they did, how discerning we are (or not) about the company that we keep? We are not threatened or persecuted as our first-century brethren were. But perhaps this makes us less careful about spending time with those who 'hate' the Father. With whom, then, do we prefer to spend our time?

A change of mood?

As the disciples walked with Jesus through the city towards the Brook Kidron in the east, there seems to have been a change in the mood of the disciples as they listened to Jesus talking intently to them. In the upper room they had been asking questions and seeking for clarification; but now Jesus notices that they have stopped asking him questions: "None of you asketh me whither goest thou?" (16:5). This is particularly significant, as "Jesus knew that they were (still) desirous to ask him" (16:19).

It may be that they felt rebuked by Jesus' responses to their earlier questions. It seems more likely, though, that they felt ashamed because they had not understood what he had said to them, so they preferred to keep silent. But silence was not the solution: Jesus was presenting them with earth-moving principles which they really needed to learn and remember. If they did not understand them now, they would certainly have greater difficulties dealing with the trauma of the next three days. Jesus addresses the problem, therefore, by asking them, "Do ye inquire among yourselves of that I said, A little while, and ye shall not see me: and again, a little while, and ye shall see me?" (16:19). He speaks to the disciples as if they have actually expressed their confusion to him. There is no hint of criticism in his words, simply a desire on his part that they should understand his meaning.

We can learn an immense amount from this approach. We often say things which are not understood, either because the person listening has difficulty grasping the point that we are making, or because we are not making the point clearly enough. The natural reaction is simply to assume that the hearer is either not really interested or not bright enough to see our point! In that kind of situation we may not bother to have our point understood, or we may rephrase our point in a tone of voice which shows that we think that the hearer is the one with the problem. Such an approach – where the speaker feels superior and the hearer is made to feel inferior – does not engender love and unity. This was not our Lord's approach; and it should not be ours either. Instead, "The servant of the Lord must not strive; but be gentle to all men, apt to teach, patient" (2 Tim. 2:24). The Lord's approach clearly worked: he was able to change the disciples' mood again, by gaining their confidence, so that, with a change of heart, his disciples were willing to acknowledge that they now understood: "Lo, now speakest thou plainly, and speakest no proverb" (Jno. 16:29). Yet in his patient approach, the Lord allowed them to think that the change had been in the way that Jesus spoke to them, rather than in their own state of mind!

Your sorrow shall be turned into joy

In John 16, we see Jesus concerned to warn the disciples that their word will not be heeded just as his has not been much listened to. It was important that they should understand this, because a time was coming when, as Jesus told them, "Ye shall weep and lament, but the world shall rejoice: and ye shall be sorrowful, but your sorrow shall be turned into joy" (16:20). They still had no idea that he was going to be crucified the next day and that they would be devastated, but that three days later he would be alive for evermore and they would be elated. And they also still needed to understand that, despite their joy at the resurrection of Jesus, they ought not to expect that those who had been

Jesus' enemies during his ministry would necessarily have a change of heart and turn to him.

The Lord had previously warned the disciples: "They shall put you out of the synagogues: yea, the time cometh, that whosoever killeth you will think that he doeth God service" (16:2). This essential warning was necessary to alert the disciples to forthcoming persecution. After Jesus' resurrection, the disciples would be fired up with enthusiasm as they sought opportunities to witness to the resurrection. But they had to be prepared to experience life-threatening opposition from the same quarters which had been opposed to Jesus himself.

The disciples, of course, during the ministry of Jesus, had been carried along by his commitment and by the enthusiasm of the common people, who "heard him gladly" (Mk. 12:37). But because he was now 'going away', Jesus had been concerned to reassure them that he was not going to leave them "comfortless" (Jno. 14:18). He was now also determined that they should "remember that (he had told them) of these things" (16:4). He assured them, too, that the joy that would be theirs (after his resurrection) would not be taken away from them (16:22).

We do well to bring to mind our own experience of enthusiasm when we were babes in Christ. We were going to tell the world all about "the truth as it is in Jesus"; but we discovered before long that the world did not want to know. Such experiences may have dulled our enthusiasm for speaking of the things that really matter. But if we have developed that state of mind, we should take note of the example of the disciples who, amidst great persecution, preached the word despite opposition and still managed to live the gospel.

Asking in Jesus' name

In John 16:23, Jesus assures his disciples: "Whatsoever ye ask the Father in my name, He will give it you". Reflecting on what it might mean to make requests to the Father in Jesus' name, it cannot surely be taken as a simple 'formula', to be used in order to ensure that our prayers are heard. By recommending the making of requests 'in his name', Jesus was most likely highlighting the relationship that ought to exist between the disciple, the Son, and the Father, where the Son is, both in theory and in practice, the "one mediator between God and men" (1 Tim. 2:5). This is true for us also: the scriptural relationship involved in being "*in*" someone or something is familiar to us already. We understand, for example, such biblical concepts as being "*in* Christ" (1 Thess. 4:16), "*in* Adam" (1 Cor. 15:22), and "*in* the flesh" (Gal. 2:20): they all speak of relationships. If we are "*in* Christ", we are related to Jesus Christ and thus to his Father. By birth we were all "*in* Adam", inheriting the first man's mortal and sin-prone nature. "*In* the flesh" is an aspect of being "in Adam": it describes both a human way of thinking and also our mortal, perishing bodies. So when we ask for anything in the name of Jesus, it is the only acceptable way for us to approach the Father in prayer, as it means that He will hear us because of our special relationship with Him through His Son.

But asking "in the name of Jesus" does not give us *carte blanche* to ask for "anything" in an unqualified way. We must "ask ... according to His will" if we expect the Father to respond to us (1 Jno. 5:14). This is tantamount to saying that we keep His commandments, thus manifesting His love. Thus, when we address the Father in prayer, we must both appreciate our relationship with Him and also accept our responsibilities. We can make prayer work for us if we reflect on how we should pray and what we ought to pray for. If we are careless in our prayers, we might well be expecting that we will be heard for our "much speaking" (Mt. 6:7) – and we are likely to be disappointed.

Behold, the hour … is now come

Having been perplexed by Jesus' words, the disciples now take comfort from the fact that they *think* that they understand him and his purpose clearly (16:30). But Jesus has to bring them down to earth again, lest they become overconfident in their partial understanding. And so he tells them the awful truth about the next twenty-four hours of his life: "Behold, the hour cometh, yea, is now come, that ye shall be scattered, every man to his own, and shall leave me alone" (16:32). The disciples did not know then, and would not know until it happened a few hours later, that these prophetic words would be fulfilled so soon.[7]

And yet, rather than making them downhearted at such a prospect as their abandonment of the Lord whom they loved, Jesus immediately tried to raise their spirits again. "But be of good cheer", he added, "I have overcome the world" (16:33) – a victory that he was determined to achieve through his constantly faithful and sinless life and through his love for his Father.

The Apostle John draws on this confidence of the Lord Jesus and from other elements of Jesus' words to his

---

7   See the later section, "They all forsook him and fled" on page 214.

disciples here, when he reminds us that "whatsoever is born of God overcometh the world: and this is the victory that overcometh the world, even our faith. Who is he that overcometh the world, but he that believeth that Jesus is the Son of God?" (1 Jno. 5:4-5). The sinless example of our Lord, and his faithfulness "even unto death" should give us the same confidence in our Father's willingness to bless us 'in the name of Jesus'.

Keep through Thine own name

After the lengthy conversations with the disciples, recorded in John 13-16, Jesus turns to his Father in prayer. The subject matter does not change. So far, in the upper room, and on the way to the Brook Kidron, Jesus has been concerned to teach his disciples about the key issue of *abiding*. And now, in his prayer to the Father, the Lord concentrates on the associated matter of *unity* – the unity between himself and the Father, and between the disciples and the Father and His Son. This unity was to be achieved by the work of the Father. Just as He had *kept* the Son, so Jesus asks that his disciples may be *kept* by the Father. And the mechanism that Jesus prays that his Father will use to achieve and cement that unity is very important for us to consider.

"Keep *through Thine own name* those whom Thou hast given me, that they may be one, as we *are*", Jesus asks his Father (Jno. 17:11). In case anyone might wonder just how exactly Jesus' disciples (ourselves included) are kept through 'God's own name', there need be no doubt as to what this means, because Jesus explains it to us, by asking his Father to continue the work that Jesus himself had started during his ministry: "While I was with them I kept them in Thy name" (17:12). The Gospel records bear eloquent witness to the care that Jesus lavished on attention to them as a loving shepherd cares for his flock. Jesus instructed them painstakingly, and corrected their errors with immense patience. In our lives today, both the Father and the Son continue that care by the guidance of God's living Word and, where necessary, by their carefully directed correction. For if we "endure chastening, God dealeth with (us) as with sons" (Heb. 12:7).

We should not, however, assume that being 'kept' by the Father guarantees that we will not fall. Jesus 'kept' the disciples; but he lost "the son of perdition" (Jno. 17:12). Judas was lost because he did not listen properly to the Word of God in person: he refused correction and went his own way, and he was finally given up by the Lord Jesus "to a reprobate mind" (Rom. 1:28). The exhortation is clear; and Scripture abounds with examples of men falling away [8] after being first delivered from "the corruption that is in the world because of sinful desire" (2 Pet. 1:4, ESV).

Being 'kept' by the Father involves our 'sanctification' (Jno. 17:17). We are 'made holy' by the work of the Father (since we cannot do the work ourselves). The law teaches us that corruption and uncleanness is passed on, while holiness is not, as the prophet Haggai confirms (2:12-13). Sanctification comes through "Thy word" (Jno. 7:17) – a confirmation of Psalm 119:9. Holiness is not an innate human quality; but it is one that can be acquired through a diligent application to the word of the Father and the teachings of His Son. And that is why the things that Jesus told his disciples in the upper room and on the way to the Brook Kidron, and which are recorded at such length by the Apostle John, are so very important:

---

8   For example, in Jude 5 and Hebrews 3:16-17.

they encapsulate and develop the teaching of Jesus during the previous three-and-a-half years of his ministry. Jesus prayed for his disciples to be 'sanctified' in his Father's name; and he wants that for us also. If we wish to be 'in that name', we must manifest 'holiness' in our lives (Mt. 5:8). We do well, therefore, to take heed to the exhortation given to us "as unto children" (Heb. 12:5), for without "holiness … no man shall see the Lord" (12:14).

At this point, Jesus and the disciples "went forth over the Brook Kidron" (Jno. 18:1), towards his final, and most difficult, time of trial. We see him crossing the Kidron and walking up the hillside into the garden, and we are amazed and humbled at the extent of his love, demonstrated in his willingness to "lay down his life for his friends" (15:13).

An insight into the prayer-life of Jesus

That Jesus spent a great deal of time in prayer is clear. We are told of occasions when he spent the whole night in prayer (for example, Luke 6:12). On other occasions, it is evident that he prayed when he had difficult issues to deal with (Jno. 6:15). But we are not privileged to hear what he said at such times. We are told how he recommended his disciples to speak to the Father in their prayers (Mt. 6:9-13; Lk. 11:2-4); and we are also given a glimpse into his prayer in Gethsemane. On that occasion it is clear that Jesus said far more than is recorded, since he asked three of his disciples, "Could ye not watch with me one hour?" (Mt. 26:40).

On the other hand, John 17 contains a long prayer which Jesus spoke in the presence of his disciples on their journey from the upper room to the Garden of Gethsemane. A consideration of what Jesus said in that prayer gives us valuable insight into the Lord's own prayer-life, and can instruct us on what should be important in our prayers to our heavenly Father.

The first thing we notice as we read the prayer of Jesus in John 17 is how remarkably selfless Jesus is. His focus is on God and on his immediate disciples. Even when he speaks of himself, it is only in relation to his Father's glory: "... glorify Thy Son that Thy Son also may glorify Thee" (17:1). Jesus does not speak of his own needs, even though he knows what the next twenty-four hours hold for him: "I pray not for the world, but for them which Thou hast given me" (17:9). Knowing the needs of the eleven [9] as a consequence of them having spent over three years with him, Jesus prays that they might be united in their purpose. On three different occasions during Jesus' ministry there had been strife among the disciples as to who would be "the greatest":

1. Shortly after the transfiguration, Luke 9:46;

2. In Capernaum after the resurrection, Mark 9:34; [10]

3. In the upper room, Luke 22:4.

Three times (Jno. 17:11, 21, 22), Jesus prays that the disciples might be "one" – 'at one', 'harmonious'. And in addition,

---

9 By this point, Jesus seems to have accepted that Judas was 'a hopeless case', since he singles Judas out as the only one of the twelve to have been lost, and calls him "the son of perdition" (17:12).

10 It might be argued that the events recorded in Luke 9:46 and Mark 9:34 are slightly different accounts of the same event. However, a close reading of the passages seems to indicate that the original dispute simmered as they journeyed to Capernaum, and this was what prompted Jesus to challenge them as they entered the house in Capernaum.

Jesus prayed that "they may be made perfect in one" (17:23). This focus is not simply because the disciples had been at strife during the ministry. Strife among them, if it continued after Jesus' ascension, would prove an obstacle to the preaching of the gospel. So Jesus prayed "that they all may be one ... that the world may believe that Thou hast sent me" (17:21). A disunited group would not effectively demonstrate that Jesus had come from God.

It is possible that believers today may manifest similar qualities to those which the disciples showed during Jesus' ministry. Jesus' desire "that the world may believe" should act as a powerful motivator as we strive for unity among ourselves. Preaching the correct doctrines, whilst essential, is only part of the work. The hardest part is living a life which reflects those doctrines. We should be very thankful that Jesus did not just pray for the eleven, but also "for them which shall believe on me through their word" (17:20).

Despite their constant presence with Jesus for over three years, the twelve displayed a lack of understanding on a number of occasions. For example: Luke 9:54 ("Shall we call down fire ...?"); or Matthew 16:11 ("How is it that ye do not understand that I spake ... not to you concerning bread, that ye should beware of the leaven of the Pharisees and of the Sadducees?"); or their slowness to appreciate that the Scriptures had foretold Jesus' triumphal entry into Jerusalem (Jno. 12:12-16). Despite these frustrations, Jesus recognised that God had given him his closest followers, and so he prays for them (17:6 – twice – 7, 9, 11).

So do we have the same appreciation of our fellow believers? Do we pray for them, that they might be at one, or that they might be kept from evil? [11] Do we regard our fellow believers as belonging to God as Jesus spoke of his followers (17:9)? Do we pray for their sanctification as Jesus did for them?

This rare insight into what Jesus asked his Father in prayer should teach us that our prayers, rather than focussing on ourselves, should focus on God and our fellow believers.

The way to Gethsemane

Matthew, Mark and Luke now converge with John on the walk from the upper room to Gethsemane. John alone has told us about the conversations and teaching of the Lord on the way over the Kidron and into the garden. Matthew and Mark tell us that Jesus went to "Gethsemane". Luke informs us that they went to the "Mount of Olives", "as he was wont" (Lk. 22:39). We may wonder how Judas Iscariot knew to go to Gethsemane to find Jesus when he returned with the "band" (Jno. 18:3). It is possible that he went back to the upper room first only to find it deserted; but this is perhaps unlikely given the number of men that Judas had with him. Jesus went "oft" to the Mount of Olives and "Gethsemane"; and this will have been enough for Judas to know where he would find Jesus and the disciples after they had left the upper room. It is also possible, of course, that Jesus actually told Judas where they would go after the meal. So Judas and the "band" arrive at Gethsemane, where Jesus already was.

John provides additional information about the journey from the upper room to Gethsemane. John writes that "he (Jesus)

---

11 Jesus' prayer for the disciples that God would "keep them from the evil" echoes what Jesus had taught them to pray for (Mt. 6:13).

went forth with his disciples over the brook Cedron" (Jno. 18:1). To get to Gethsemane from the city, anyone would have to cross over the Kidron; but John mentions the fact purposely. This detail draws attention to the way in which king David left Jerusalem during the uprising of Absalom. The account in Samuel records that "the king also himself passed over the brook Kidron" (2 Sam. 15:23). This is the only other place in Scripture where this phrase occurs. We notice the beginning of a series of links with this time in David's life.

But there is not simply this repetition of a key phrase to highlight the similarity between the actions of David and Jesus. A contrast between the two events is also highlighted in the way that the journeys are described. Of Jesus it is said that "he went forth with his disciples over the brook Cedron, where was a *garden*" (Jno. 18:1), whereas of David's journey we read that he went "toward the way of the *wilderness*" (2 Sam. 15:23). This contrast marks the different expectations of the two men. Whereas David did not know the outcome of his flight and he was therefore heading towards a bleak future, Jesus knew that he was making a purposeful journey which would have his resurrection as its terminus. Hence, he "entered" the garden (Jno. 18:1); and his disciples went in with him, typifying the fact that, not only Jesus himself, but also those who believed in him, were encompassed within the saving work that Jesus was shortly to accomplish.

The Garden of Gethsemane

The Garden of Gethsemane was an orchard of vines. It will have been a walled garden, probably with a winepress. The enclosing wall would serve to protect the vines from the wind and the grapes from theft by the local inhabitants. We should not presume, because Jesus went to Gethsemane at night, that Jerusalem itself would have been quiet. This was Passover time, after all – a feast at which all males were to "appear before the LORD ... in the place which He shall choose" (Deut. 16:16). At that time, therefore, Jerusalem would be packed with visiting pilgrims staying over for the feast. On an earlier occasion Jesus and his family travelled up to Jerusalem with friends and neighbours (Lk. 2:42-44), so we know that this aspect of the Law of Moses was observed by at least some in Israel in those days. Such an influx of people will have placed great pressure on accommodation within the city, and many will have camped around the city in the fields and on the hillsides. In the Kidron valley, therefore, and on the slopes of the Mount of Olives, many families unable to find lodgings in the city or who could not afford such accommodation would be camping. Jesus and his disciples must have passed such family groups on their way to Gethsemane.

But once inside the garden, things would be quiet, providing an ideal environment for Jesus and his disciples. For Jesus, because there was no one to distract him. For the disciples, because it provided security for them and a place to rest. As a walled garden it would provide Jesus and his disciples with a quiet place of solitude amidst the bustle of Passover in and around Jerusalem.

Events	Matthew	Mark	Luke	John	Time
Jesus arrives in Gethsemane	26:36	14:32	22:39	18:1	Night
Jesus takes three disciples	26:37	14:33			

Events	Matthew	Mark	Luke	John	Time
The prayers in Gethsemane	26:39-44	14:35-41	22:41-46		

A review of this table demonstrates that, whereas John's record provides much information about the meal in the upper room and unique information about the journey from the upper room to Gethsemane, it is silent as far as the events in the garden are concerned.

Old Testament parallels and the use of Old Testament language

This time in Jesus' life is deeply reminiscent of the time of the rebellion of Absalom in the life of David. The Gospels appear to be deliberately highlighting a number of parallels between the Lord's betrayal by Judas in Gethsemane and that time of testing in David's life. We need to be sensitive to these links because they are preserved in Scripture so that we might appreciate how Jesus took considerable comfort from the way in which his Father delivered David in his time of great distress. Judas answers to Ahithophel, whilst the chief priests correspond to Absalom and Jesus to David. [12]

Geographically, the Garden of Gethsemane can be described as being on the Mount of Olives, which is how

---

[12] Parallels between Judas and Ahithophel have already been seen during the meal in the upper room (see especially Appendix 2, "Bible echoes: David's flight from Absalom" on page 224). A similar theme continues into the language used about events in the Garden of Gethsemane.

Luke describes it (Lk. 22:39). But there is a particular reason for this description in Luke. When David fled from Absalom he "went up by the ascent of Mount Olivet" (2 Sam. 15:30). Luke is highlighting a link between David's flight from Absalom and the Lord's 'ascent' of the Mount of Olives to Gethsemane. Luke's use of language from the Samuel record sets the scene for the other links with David's flight from Jerusalem which follow:

Quotations from the Old Testament as Jesus prayed in Gethsemane			
John 18:1	over Cedron	2 Samuel 15:23	over Kidron
Matthew 26:37	heavy	Psalm 69:20	full of heaviness
		Psalm 119:28	heaviness
Matthew 26:38	sorrowful even unto death	Psalm 42:6	soul is cast down
Mark 14:36; Luke 22:42	nevertheless not what I will, but what Thou wilt	2 Samuel 15:26	let Him do ... as seemeth good unto Him
Mark 14:37	couldest not thou watch ... ?	Psalm 69:20	looked ... for comforters ... found none
Luke 22:39	Mount of Olives	2 Samuel 15:30	Mount of Olives
Luke 22:41	stone's cast	2 Samuel 16:6	cast stones
Luke 22:43	angel	Psalm 91:11	give his angels charge
Luke 22:43	strengthening	Psalm 119:28	strengthen
Luke 22:49	shall we smite with the sword?	2 Samuel 16:9	let me ... take off his head

These quotations are from Scriptures relating to David's flight from Absalom. Reviewing the Scriptures used can help us to focus on the pathos of our Lord's situation.

Heavy and sorrowful

Both Matthew (26:37) and Mark (14:33) say that Jesus became "heavy" with the sorrow of his situation. With the use of these expressions by the Gospel writers, we begin to feel something of the desperate state that Jesus was in; and the language used clearly points us to see Jesus' association with David's flight from Absalom near the end of his life.

Psalm 69, for example, speaks in prophecy about the events of Jesus' ministry (v. 9), his agony in Gethsemane (v. 20), the sleeping disciples in Gethsemane (v. 20), the crucifixion (v. 21), and the demise of Judas Iscariot and the need for a replacement (v. 25). The Psalm also speaks of David's circumstances when Absalom tried to take the kingdom to himself with the help of Ahithophel, the man who had been David's trusted counsellor. Being "full of heaviness" (Ps. 69:20) catches David's feelings at that time. He had been rejected by the people, for "Absalom stole the hearts of the men of Israel" (2 Sam. 15:6). In like manner Jesus was "despised and rejected of men" (Isa. 53:3). Jesus' "sorrow" (Mt. 26:38) picks up the phrase "a man of sorrows" (Isa. 53:3) and further highlights the way in which Isaiah 53 also speaks of this time in Jesus' life.

A stone's cast

That Jesus "was withdrawn about a stone's cast" (Lk. 22:41) from his faithful disciples, seems a very casual way of describing his separation from the three that he chose to be near him. But in fact it catches the behaviour of Shimei, who "cast stones at David" (2 Sam. 16:7) as the king fled from before Absalom. So *why* does the Spirit make this link? Perhaps because Shimei's behaviour was representative of all of David's enemies, and was an indication of the abject position that David was in, with his favourite son rising up against him. Similarly, those who only four days earlier had cried "Hosanna to the Son of David: Blessed is he that cometh in the name of the Lord; Hosanna in the highest" (Mt. 21:9), would be crying the next day: "Crucify him" (Mk. 15:13). It is as if they were casting stones at Jesus, reproachfully taunting him, as Shimei taunted David.

Selecting prayer companions

Jesus entered the garden with the eleven remaining disciples, who were left to sit and wait while Jesus went to pray (Mt. 26:36; Mk. 14:32). However, for his intense session of prayer, he took with him Peter, James and John (14:33), separating himself and these three from the rest of the disciples. There were three occasions when these three disciples were taken by Jesus and separated from the rest of the disciples; and these are tabulated below:

Event	Matthew	Mark	Luke
Raising of Jairus' daughter		5:37	8:51
Transfiguration	17:1	9:2	9:28
Gethsemane	26:37	14:33	

It was also this same group of three who came to Jesus, along with Andrew, with questions about the destruction of the temple in the Olivet Prophecy (Mk. 13:3). It may have been the fact that Jesus had already singled out Peter, James and John to witness the raising of Jairus' daughter and the Transfiguration that motivated them to "come unto [Jesus], saying, Master, we would that thou shouldest do for us whatsoever we shall desire" (10:35). But whatever the reason for this request, one thing is sure: these three disciples had been privy to some very special experiences. Yet in Gethsemane, the magnitude of the events they were witnessing escaped them and they slept, despite the fact that Jesus had asked them to "watch with (him)" (Mt. 26:38).

Jesus then moved some distance away from the three, having told them to "Pray that (they) enter not into temptation" (Lk. 22:40). We may wonder why, having separated the three to be with him, he withdrew from them before beginning his most intense and personal prayers. Perhaps there is something for us to learn about grief and comfort from this little detail. Those in anguish feel the need for comfort from those near to them, but they also need their own privacy. Picturing the scene, therefore, we have three disciples sitting in the moonlit night, with Jesus visible to them and praying earnestly.

Jesus prays and his disciples sleep

The three synoptic Gospels record details of Jesus' prayers in Gethsemane. John, on the other hand, makes no mention of the Lord's most anguished prayers:

Piecing together the three accounts of Jesus' prayers in Gethsemane

	Event	Matthew	Mark	Luke
1	Jesus knew that all things were possible for his Father		14:36	
2	Jesus wanted the cup to pass – he did not want to die	26:39	14:36	22:42
3	Jesus wanted to do his Father's will	26:39	14:36	22:42
4	Jesus returned to find the disciples asleep	26:40	14:37	

	Event	Matthew	Mark	Luke
5	Jesus reproved Peter	26:40-41	14:36-37	
7	Jesus was strengthened by an angel			22:43
8	He went away a second time	26:42	14:39	
9	If the cup may not pass ...	26:42		
10	Jesus returned to find the disciples asleep again	26:43	14:40	
11	Leaving the disciples Jesus returned to prayer	26:44		
12	Jesus prayed the same words a third time	26:44		
13	Jesus prayed more earnestly – with sweat as drops of blood			22:44
14	Jesus returned to find the disciples asleep again	26:45	14:41	22:45
15	Jesus told the disciples to rest	26:45	14:41	
16	Jesus woke the disciples to tell them to pray			22:46
17	'Let us rise – the betrayer is here'	26:46	14:42	22:47

From this composite account of the three Gospels which record details of the Lord's prayers in Gethsemane, we learn that on three separate occasions Jesus found the disciples asleep when he needed their support. We do not know what he said to those disciples on each of these three occasions; nor can we know how he would have been comforted by their alertness – but we can be sure that he would have received comfort in some way. Yet they failed him on each occasion.

Two days earlier, Jesus had told his disciples a number of parables on the Mount of Olives, one of which was about the ten virgins (Mt. 25:1). All ten virgins slept at night until the bridegroom came, when they woke from their sleep to find that five of them were not prepared. So perhaps the parable came to the disciples' minds in Gethsemane. Certainly, their lack of preparedness caused the Lord to say to them: "Why sleep ye? rise and pray, lest ye enter into temptation" (Lk. 22:46). We might, of course, think that being asleep prevents us being tempted; and when we are stressed we may well find that the most helpful way to cope is to go to bed to seek the forgetfulness of sleep. But Jesus' antidote to such pressures was prayer, not sleep; and he knew only too well that they would soon be sorely tempted, and they needed to pray. Peter was a case in point; for only a short while after this advice from Jesus, he tried to resist the Lord's arrest and, "having a sword (Peter) drew it, and smote the high priest's servant, and cut off his right ear" (Jno. 18:10). In this incident we see that Jesus' disciples were not as disciplined as David's men, for when he was fleeing from Absalom his men said: "Behold, thy servants are ready to do whatsoever my Lord the king shall appoint" (2 Sam. 15:15); and when Shimei cursed David, Abishai said: "Let me go over, I pray thee, and take off his head" (16:9). But at least Abishai waited for David's permission and was constrained by David saying, "So let him curse" (2 Sam. 16:10).

We need to reflect, therefore, on how our inattentiveness may be the cause of someone else suffering by our neglect. We have a responsibility to be "there" for our brethren and sisters during their times of need. We can help them in real practical ways, even if we are separated from them by distance. We can let them know that they are in our thoughts and prayers. We can express our willingness to talk with them at any time of day or night. We must be aware also that, like the disciples in Gethsemane who, on waking from their sleep, proceeded to provide the wrong kind of support, we can sometimes do more harm than good if our actions are rushed or not properly thought through.

Jesus under stress

Jesus, like Elias, was "a man subject to like passions as we are" (Jas. 5:17). He was "in all points tempted like as we are". The way in which he differed from us is that his temptation was "without sin" (Heb. 4:15). We must therefore conclude that when Jesus prayed, "O my Father, if it be possible, let this cup pass from me" (Mt. 26:39), he really meant what he said. The great conflict that Jesus experienced within himself was not simply that he did not want to die on the cross. He had the additional pressure that he knew that what he was asking did not fit with his Father's will; hence the conclusion: "Nevertheless not as I will, but as Thou wilt". Jesus' conflict was all the greater, too, because he really did believe that "all things are possible unto (God)" (Mk. 14:36).

From the three accounts of Jesus' prayer, we learn that he "fell on his face" (Mt. 26:39), "fell to the ground" (Mk. 14:35), and "kneeled down" (Lk. 22:41). This is not formal standing, or sitting, with head bowed and hands together in the comfort of a meeting room or a house. Nor were his actions mere show. Because he was "in agony" (20:44), his posture would involuntarily reflect his innermost feelings. That "his sweat was as it were great drops of blood falling down to the ground" (22:44), speaks graphically of the stress that our Lord was experiencing. Perhaps we can recall perspiration on our brows and under our arms when we have been anxious about some medical situation – a painful injection, or the removal of a tooth. Magnify that apprehension until the sweat is like "great drops of blood falling to the ground", and we may just gain an insight into the stress that the Lord was enduring at that time.

"Gethsemane" means 'winepress'. How appropriate that the Son of God experienced the pressure of his sorest trial in that very place! His sweat seems to answer to the crushing of the grapes in a winepress ("as it were great drops of blood falling down"). But Gethsemane was not "the great winepress of the wrath of God" (Rev. 14:19). Instead, the Father was bringing forth fruit from His Son, whose stress came from making his will match that of his Father. The battle that raged in the mind of Jesus was the battle between the mind of the flesh and the mind of the spirit.

But what did Jesus say?

When David fled from Jerusalem at the time of Absalom's uprising, "Zadok also, and all the Levites were with him, (bringing) the ark of the covenant of God: and they set down the ark of God" before David (2 Sam. 15:24). David, however, told them to "Carry back the ark of God into the city" (15:25). In doing this David showed his complete trust in his God. Not that he knew that he would return to the city, but that he was willing to place his confidence in God. He continues: "… if I shall find favour in the eyes of the LORD, He will bring me again, and shew me both it, and His habitation: But if He thus say, I have no delight in thee; behold, here am I, let Him do to me as seemeth good unto Him" (15:25-26). This mindset was also seen in Jesus in his prayers in the Garden of Gethsemane, when he says, "… nevertheless not my will, but Thine, be done" (Lk. 22:42). Jesus reflected on the way in which his father David responded to the treachery of Ahithophel and the rebellion of his own son Absalom. He took comfort from the way in which Yahweh took care of David and he was encouraged to continue to trust his Father. Jesus provides a wonderful example in this for us to emulate, as in all things. If we can identify with faithful individuals in Scripture in this way, they will show us how we may overcome our own problems.

Praying three times

While he was in Gethsemane, Jesus moved apart from Peter, James and John on three separate occasions to pray (Mt. 26:39, 42, 44). And, lest we should miss the point, Matthew is careful to say "second" and "third time". But _why_ did Jesus pray three times?

There are other occasions in Scripture where men of God prayed in this way about a particular problem. With respect to his "thorn in the flesh", the Apostle Paul "besought the Lord thrice, that it might depart from (him)" (2 Cor. 12:8). On three separate occasions, the prophet Jeremiah was _told not to pray_ for Israel (Jer. 7:16; 11:14; and 14:11) – which clearly indicates that he had been praying for his people, even though he had been foretelling their destruction. So maybe this kind of frequency is a recommended pattern of prayer for us to follow: make your request known three times and then leave things in God's hand.

Looking for comforters

The disciples slept while Jesus needed their support. This echoes David's feelings of despair during Absalom's uprising. Psalm 69 was clearly written against the background of that upheaval. In the Psalm, David's anxieties and concerns are expressed, and his personal feelings are exposed to public view. "I am full of heaviness", he says, "and I looked for some to take pity, but there was none; and for comforters, but I found none" (Ps. 69:20). Jesus looked to his disciples for some support; but he found them sleeping ("could ye not watch with me one hour?", Matthew 26:40). [13] Clearly, what both David and Jesus needed was not just human sympathy, but some real encouragement and genuine fellowship in their suffering.

While Jesus looked for comfort – the fellowship of companions – from Peter, James and John, they were actually no support to him at all. So instead, "there appeared an angel unto him from heaven, strengthening him" (Lk. 22:43). Jesus had told his disciples that he would not leave them comfortless (Jno. 14:18). In like manner, the Lord God did not leave His Son without comfort; and the mere presence of the angel would be a powerful encouragement to Jesus to know that he was not alone in his time of trial. But perhaps, if Peter, James and John had not slept, the angel would not have been required.

There are powerful implications for us in these experiences of David and the Lord Jesus. In both sets of circumstances, there was little that man could do to make the situation very much better. David doubtless saw the rebellion of Absalom as a fulfilment of Nathan's words in 2 Samuel 12:11-12: "Thus saith the LORD, Behold, I will raise up evil against thee out of thine own house, and I will take thy wives

---

13 The expression "to take pity" (Ps. 69:20, AV) means '*to lament with me*' in the Hebrew.

before thine eyes, and give them unto thy neighbour, and he shall lie with thy wives in the sight of this sun". Jesus knew that if his Father's will was to be done, the cup could not pass. Both men had to resolve their own problems, but they needed the presence of faithful friends to provide comfort and support.

Comfort from an angel [14]

We might wonder *when* the angel appeared. Was it after the first, second or third session of prayer? We might think that we cannot know the answer to this question. However, a little thought may cause us to conclude that the angel's visit was after Jesus returned to prayer when he found the disciples asleep for the first time, as suggested in the last table above. Jesus had asked Peter, James and John to sit while he went and prayed "yonder" (Mt. 26:36); but they fell asleep, for when he returned he found them asleep (26:40). It appears that on this occasion, Jesus was somewhat distressed: "Could ye not watch? Watch and pray that ye enter not into temptation" (26:40-41). On the second time that Jesus returned and found them asleep (26:43), he left them and returned to prayer. Jesus was then at a point where he was in particular need of support. He had hoped to receive it from his disciples; but they were asleep – so instead of encouraging him by their presence they frustrated him by their sleep. Consider. Jesus was in agony, praying that he would have the resolve to submit to his Father's will, in order that he might bring salvation to mankind. But on his return, three of those he was working to save were asleep! So the Father sent an angel who

---

14 Thanks are due to Brother Andrew E. Walker for provoking comments and providing the basic data for this section.

"strengthened him" (Lk. 22:43), at the point when Jesus was perhaps at his lowest ebb.

Whilst the record is silent as to *how* the angel strengthened Jesus, we can nevertheless form a helpful conclusion as to what took place. The form of words in Luke 22:43 ("strengthening him") provides an insight into what might have passed between the angel and Jesus. There is clearly more than an allusion here to Psalm 119:28 ("My soul melteth for heaviness: strengthen Thou me according unto Thy word"), which may suggest that the angel spoke to Jesus about the Scriptures concerning his mission. [15] There is certainly no indication of some miraculous power being given to Jesus, and this experience of Jesus provides a pattern for us. Our understanding of the way that God is working in our lives comes from a correct understanding of the word of God – not from some 'inner feeling' of strength. The strength comes from appreciating anew what the Father is doing in our lives and for us.

Providing comfort today

The Father will provide the comfort and support that His children need. He can do this without our help, of course; but it is better for us if He uses us to comfort others in times of need. We show our love for God in the way that we respond to the needs of our brethren and sisters. The way that we respond to them is taken by the Lord as a response to him: "And the King shall answer and say unto them, Verily I say unto you, Inasmuch as ye have done it unto

---

15 This would not be unlike the strengthening effect that Moses and Elijah had on Jesus during the Transfiguration, when they "spake of his decease which he should accomplish at Jerusalem" (Lk. 9:31).

one of the least of these my brethren, ye have done it unto me" (Mt. 25:40). Or again, if we cannot show love to our brethren and sisters, neither can we love God: "If a man say, I love God, and hateth his brother, he is a liar: for he that loveth not his brother whom he hath seen, how can he love God whom he hath not seen?" (1 Jno. 4:20). Such care and love can be show with a card, a phone call or a short visit. Just to know that we are in the thoughts of others during times of need is a great comfort.

Rise, let us be going

After Jesus had spent time in prayer, he returned and found the disciples sleeping once again. There must have been a period of time between Jesus' return to the disciples and the arrival of Judas, since the Gospel records imply that Jesus both encouraged the disciples to sleep, and also to rise and be ready to leave because the betrayer was at hand:

- *Matthew 26:45-46* – "Then cometh he to his disciples, and saith unto them, Sleep on now, and take your rest: [...] behold, the hour is at hand, and the Son of man is betrayed into the hands of sinners. Rise, let us be going: behold, he is at hand that doth betray me".

- *Mark 14:41-42* – "And he cometh the third time, and saith unto them, Sleep on now, and take your rest: it is enough, the hour is come; behold, the Son of man is betrayed into the hands of sinners. [...] Rise up, let us go; lo, he that betrayeth me is at hand".

The square bracket in each passage [...] indicates the time gap. We have no way of knowing how long that gap was; but the record still permits us to see again the compassion of Jesus at work. Aware of what was to follow, and the impact it would have on the disciples, Jesus allowed them to sleep on and rest, even though these were the same men from whom he had looked for comfort at an earlier stage. [16]

The arrest of Jesus

Comparing the four accounts of the group that came to arrest Jesus is most instructive:

- *Matthew 26:47* – "And while he yet spake, lo, Judas, one of the twelve, came, and with him a great multitude with swords and staves, from the chief priests and elders of the people".

- *Mark 14:43* – "And immediately, while he yet spake, cometh Judas, one of the twelve, and with him a great multitude with swords and staves, from the chief priests and the scribes and the elders".

- *Luke 22:47* – "And while he yet spake, behold a multitude, and he that was called Judas, one of the twelve, went before them, and drew near unto Jesus to kiss him".

- *John 18:3* – "Judas then, having received a band of men and officers from the chief priests and Pharisees, cometh thither with lanterns and torches and weapons".

Judas features in all four of these records. But there is no mention of the chief priests actually being there. In fact, the record in Matthew, Mark, and John say that the group came "*from* the chief priests". It is John who specifically says that Judas "received a band" (18:3). So Judas was the

---

16 It is clear from the records that Jesus spoke twice with an interval between the two occasions.

ringleader in the arresting party! In this respect he answers to Ahithophel who, when speaking to Absalom, said "Let *me* now choose out twelve thousand men, and *I* will arise ... And *I* will come upon him" (2 Sam. 17:1-2). No doubt the chief priests were of the same mind as Absalom, of whom it is said, "And the saying pleased Absalom well, and all the elders of Israel" (17:4).

The order of events around the arrest of Jesus

Event	Matthew	Mark	Luke	John
The band arrive	26:47	14:43	22:47	18:3
Judas kisses Jesus	26:49	14:45	22:47	–
Jesus questions Judas	26:50	–	22:48	–
1st Who are you seeking?	–	–	–	18:4
Accusers go "backward"	–	–	–	18:6
2nd Who are you seeking?	–	–	–	18:7
Jesus requests that the disciples be allowed to leave	–	–	–	18:8
Jesus arrested	26:50	14:46	–	–
Disciples ask 'shall we smite with the sword?'	–	–	22:49	–
Malchus' ear cut off	26:51	14:47	22:50	18:10
I can ask for angels	26:53	–	–	–
I must drink the cup given by my Father	–	–	–	18:11
Malchus' ear healed	–	–	22:51	–
Jesus speaks to the multitude	26:55	14:49-49	22:52-53	–
The disciples flee	26:56	14:50	–	–
Jesus is bound and taken from the Garden	26:57	14:53	22:54	18:12

As Jesus was speaking to the disciples (Mt. 26:47; Mk. 14:43; Lk. 22:47), the great crowd led by Judas (Mt. 26:47) arrived to take Jesus, armed with "swords and staves" (26:47; Mk. 14:43) and "lanterns and torches" (Jno. 18:3). The word "band" (18:3) answers to the military term *cohort* in the Roman army, a cohort being a group of six hundred men. [17] We might well wonder what the chief priests and rulers expected from Jesus – they clearly did not know what kind of man he was, but they were afraid of his power. Yet when his disciples asked him, "Lord, wilt thou that we command fire to come down from heaven, and consume them, even as Elias did?" (Lk. 9:54), Jesus' response was: "Ye know not what manner of spirit ye are of. For the Son of man is not come to destroy men's lives, but to save them" (9:55-56). Jesus was not surprised by the arrival of the great crowd. He will have seen them snaking across the Kidron valley from the city, with their lanterns and torches. David, too, when fleeing from Absalom, said: "I will not be afraid of ten thousands of people, that have set themselves against me round about" (Ps. 3:6); and this may well have provided Jesus with an insight into what to expect when he was arrested.

Judas had already planned with those whom he had brought to take Jesus, saying, "Whomsoever I shall kiss, that same is he: hold him fast" (Mt. 26:48); but before Judas had an opportunity to effect his plan, Jesus took control of the situation by asking: "Whom seek ye?" (Jno. 18:4). His further response ("I am he", 18:5), took them all aback, for they "went backward, and fell to the ground" (18:6). Some have

---

17 Greek, *speira*(n): 'a military cohort', 'the tenth part of a legion' (*i.e.* about 600 legionaries), 'either 500 or 1,000 men, if auxiliaries', or 'a maniple, the thirtieth part of a legion'.

suggested that they "went backward" because Jesus used the divine name; but there may be a different explanation. In Psalm 40 we read: "Let them be ashamed and confounded together that seek after my soul to destroy it; let them be *driven backward* and put to shame that wish me evil" (v. 14). We know that Psalm 40 is prophetic of Jesus' work: verses 6-8 are quoted in Hebrews 10:5-9 and applied to the commitment Jesus showed to serving his Father. As for Judas himself, he still "stood" with Jesus' antagonists (Jno. 18:5); and his behaviour demonstrated where he was, spiritually, for he was standing "in the way of sinners" (Ps. 1:1). His fate was now sealed, for "the way of the ungodly shall perish" (1:6).

The reaction of Jesus' enemies prompted him to ask again: "Whom seek ye?" (Jno. 18:7); and once more they responded with words rather than actions! Try to visualise the scene: there are 12 men in the garden and more than 600 more arrive to capture one of them. One among the six hundred has agreed to identify the one to be taken, while the one being sought takes control of the situation and asks a question which, to say the least, disarms his antagonists to such an extent that he has to ask the same question again. The response of the antagonists is simply, twice, to give the name of the man they are seeking. And while all this is going on the betrayer stands by watching!

There was, of course, a reason why Jesus took the initiative in this situation – and it was not to preserve his own life, for he continues: "I have told you that I am he: if therefore ye seek me, let these go their way" (18:8). Jesus was concerned for the wellbeing of his disciples! He had prayed to his Father that he might lose none of his disciples (17:12); and now he was working to ensure that his prayer would be answered. There is a lesson in this for us. Simply praying to God and sitting back to wait for His response is not enough. Jesus prayed, and then did what he could to ensure that his request could be granted. In the same way, we ought actively to pursue the thing we have requested.

It was at this point that Judas "came to Jesus, and said, Hail, Master; and kissed him" (Mt. 26:49). For Judas, Jesus was still Master/Teacher, but not Lord. This was how Judas had responded in the upper room, when Jesus told all the disciples that one of them would betray him (26:21). The other disciples, by contrast, had called Jesus their Lord:

- *Matthew 26:22* – "And they were exceeding sorrowful, and began every one of them to say unto him, <u>Lord</u>, is it I?"

- *Matthew 26:25* – "Then Judas, which betrayed him, answered and said, <u>Master</u>, is it I? He said unto him, Thou hast said".

Judas and Ahithophel

It is perhaps too easy to dogmatise about the motives of Judas in betraying his Master. But there are undoubtedly pre-echoes of his motivation and expectations to be found in the life of David when he fled from his son Absalom and his trusted counsellor Ahithophel. And this is not speculation, since Jesus himself drew a parallel between Judas and Ahithophel when, speaking of his betrayer in the upper room, he quoted Psalm 41:9 – a verse directly referring to Ahithophel [18] – and said (of Judas): "That the

---

18 Psalm 41:9 – "Yea, mine own familiar friend, in whom I trusted, <u>which did eat of my bread, hath lifted up his heel against me</u>".

Scripture may be fulfilled, *He that eateth bread with me hath lifted up his heel against me*" (Jno. 13:18).

David fleeing from Absalom		Jesus in Gethsemane	
2 Samuel 15:31	David's "familiar friend" with Absalom	Matthew 26:47	Judas with those opposing Jesus

The way in which the Gospel records present Jesus as following in the steps of his father David is designed to make us realise that Jesus used the events of the Old Testament to help him to decide how he should behave. This is not to say that Jesus would simply copy David's behaviour, or that his behaviour had been determined beforehand. Instead, Jesus learned from Scripture how his Father would want him to behave, by examining the lives of others contained in God's word.

There comes a time when we know the Father's will but struggle to keep it. We have said all we can in prayer. We have done all that it is possible for us to do. In such a circumstance we, like Jesus, might do well to pray 'saying the same words'. We know that the Father heard his son's groanings, because of the angel sent to strengthen him (Lk. 22:43). So for us, whilst we cannot see the angel, we can still have the same confidence that "if we ask any thing according to His will, He heareth us" (1 Jno. 5:14). Jesus knew the outcome of the events in David's flight from before Absalom: David was brought back safely into the city. Being able to identify with his father David provided Jesus, in this time of great stress, with a role model to copy. We do well to identify the faithful men and women in Scripture, as Jesus did.

Friend

These are the only three uses of the word "friend" (Greek, *hetaire*) in the New Testament: in Matthew 20:13; 22:12 and 26:50. The first two are in parables towards the end of Jesus' life, whilst the third is used in Jesus' response to Judas' kiss in Gethsemane. In the two parables, the "friend" is one who has been involved in the work (20:13) and one who has been bidden to the marriage (22:12). But neither of these friends lives up to the expectations of the one who uses the term. In Matthew 20 the labourer is not satisfied with what he has agreed to; and in Matthew 22 the "friend" had not prepared himself for the feast to which he had been called. In using this comparatively rare word to address Judas in Gethemane, therefore, it is highly likely that Jesus was trying to draw Judas' attention to the two parables that he had recently spoken. Judas, in other words, shared the characteristics of the two 'friends' who had already failed to come up to expectations. Coming from Jesus to Judas in this particular context, the word "friend" was a form of veiled reproof from Master to disciple.

But there is more to this word "friend" than this link with the parables. We have already seen that it was the parallel between the "familiar friend" of Psalm 41:9 which Jesus applied to Judas (Jno. 13:18). Psalm 55 provides even greater detail about the failure of the close relationship that had once existed between David and his counsellor Ahithophel:

> "For it was not an enemy that reproached me; then I could have borne it: neither was it he that hated me that did magnify himself against me; then I would have hid myself from him: But it was thou, a man mine equal, my

guide, and mine acquaintance. We took sweet counsel together, and walked unto the house of God in company ... The words of his mouth were smoother than butter, but war was in his heart: his words were softer than oil, yet were they drawn swords" (Ps. 55:11-14, 21).

From this Psalm we learn that:

- David did not regard Ahithophel as an enemy.
- David viewed Ahithophel as his "equal", so valuable was his guidance and counsel.
- They worshipped together.
- Ahithophel spoke smooth, but deceitful words.

We are invited to conclude that this was the kind of relationship that had existed between Jesus and Judas. So Judas may well have been one of the disciples who seemed quite spiritual, and who gave every appearance of being close to Jesus. And perhaps, therefore, in using the word "friend" to Judas, Jesus was trying to make him reflect on Ahithophel, his Old Testament counterpart. There is certainly a grim irony in the fact that both Ahithophel and Judas committed suicide by hanging (2 Sam. 17:23; Mt. 27:5).

Judas and Balaam

In other ways, too, the behaviour of Judas mirrored that of Balaam, as a short table of links suggests:

Numbers 22:7	"the wages of unrighteousness"/"the reward of iniquity"	Acts 1:18
Numbers 22:32	"thy way is perverse"/"fallen headlong"	Acts 1:18

Speaking of Balaam's motivation for his actions, Peter informs us that Balaam "loved the wages of unrighteousness" (2 Pet. 2:15), which corresponds with his description of the "reward of iniquity" received by Judas (Acts 1:18). And the angel of the LORD says of Balaam's behaviour that it is "perverse" (Num. 22:32, AV), where the Hebrew *yarat* means, literally, 'precipitate', and matches up with the sense of the word "headlong" in Acts 1:18, where the sense of the Greek *prenes* is 'downwards, at speed'.

These links are most useful for, along with the links between Judas and Ahithophel, they provide a scripturally-based insight into what it was that motivated Judas to betray Jesus. Ahithophel wanted David out of the way, and saw Absalom as 'the coming man' and therefore the route through which this could be achieved. His desire was completely self-centered, as can be seen in the repeated use of the first person pronoun "I" by Ahithophel in 2 Samuel 17:1-3. Balaam, on the other hand, was simply concerned with the money. So greedy was he that when he was unable to curse Israel, he still found a way to cause Israel "to commit trespass against the LORD in the matter of Peor" (Num. 31:16). In the same way that we are unable to attribute good motives to either Balaam or Ahithophel, we conclude that it is also not possible to impute 'good' motives to Judas when he betrayed Jesus.

Kissing Jesus

Luke informs us (22:47) that Judas came to Jesus intending to kiss him, as this was the signal that Judas had pre-arranged for Jesus' arrest, to make sure the correct man was taken. And despite being reproved by Jesus, Judas nevertheless went on to kiss Jesus anyway. Matthew and Mark use the same words to describe Judas' actions; and they both use a word for "kiss" which indicates that Judas kissed Jesus more than once":

- *Matthew 26:49* – "Kissed him" (Greek, "kissed him much").
- *Mark 14:45* – "Kissed him" (Greek, "kissed him much").

This brings Proverbs 27:6 to mind: "Faithful are the wounds of a friend; but the kisses of an enemy are deceitful". Jesus knew what Judas had in mind; so, in challenging him, Jesus was encouraging Judas to reflect upon what he was about to do. The problem for Judas was that he was set on a course of action and was, so to speak, proceeding 'perversely'/'headlong' to his destruction.

The disciples and swords

By the time Jesus had arrived at Gethsemane he knew that they had with them, not one, but two swords. In response to Jesus' statement in Luke 22:36 ("But now ... he that hath no sword, let him sell his garment, and buy one"), they had said, "Lord, behold, here are two swords" (22:38). So what was Jesus recommending? He cannot have been encouraging the disciples to adopt the use of force, since this was completely alien to him. In his first major preaching effort, he had taught his hearers to "resist not evil: but whosoever shall smite thee on thy right cheek, turn to him the other also" (Mt. 5:39). When James and John had thought to call down fire on their enemies (Lk. 9:54), Jesus "turned, and rebuked them, and said, Ye know not what manner of spirit ye are of" (9:55); and he taught that "the Son of man is not come to destroy men's lives" (9:56). His concern was the salvation of men, not their destruction. Later still he would say to Pilate: "My kingdom is not of this world: if my kingdom were of this world, then would my servants fight, that I should not be delivered to the Jews" (Jno. 18:36). So we learn that the disciples of Jesus are pacifists, if only conditional ones. They will not fight for this world, which "passeth away" (1 Cor. 7:31; 1 Jno. 2:17), but only for the kingdom of Christ when it descends with him from heaven. Jesus had been teaching this doctrine for over three years, and yet the disciples still did not understand, which no doubt explains why Jesus responded, "It is enough" (Lk. 22:38). [19]

Anticipating what was going to happen to Jesus, the disciples asked him: "Lord, shall we smite with the sword?" (22:49). But without waiting for the answer, Peter "drew his sword, and struck a servant of the high priest, and smote off his ear" (Mt. 26:51). It is possible that Peter was actually aiming at Judas, seeking to do him some injury, and that Malchus was simply the hapless individual who was in the way of Peter's attack. Up to this point, the band who had come to capture Jesus had simply been watching the exchanges; but it seems that they were now galvanised into

---

[19] It is not possible to be dogmatic as to whether by "It is enough" Jesus meant 'two swords will be sufficient' (which seems unlikely, given that no necessary uses for two swords are specified elsewhere), or 'That's enough of that!' (which seems more likely in relation to Jesus' consistent stand on non-violence, but it is not entirely borne out by the grammar and/or syntax of the Greek). It seems highly likely, however, given the disciples' track-record of misunderstanding of Jesus' meaning, that they had not properly understood what he meant in Luke 22:36 in the first place!

action by Peter's behaviour – after all, they had been brought along just in case there was any trouble, or resistance. But amid the confusion that doubtless arose from the attack on Malchus, Jesus took control again, by touching Malchus' ear and healing it (Lk. 22:51). At the same time, he reminded the disciples that "all they that take the sword shall perish with the sword" (Mt. 26:52).

A further test for Jesus

It seems that the leaders were not worried about the disciples, nor apparently determined to arrest them. Perhaps they feared Jesus so much that they considered it possible that Jesus might 'call down fire', as Elijah had done, or invoke some other actions in order to deliver himself. They would not have been wrong to think in this way, for Jesus said to Peter: "Thinkest thou that I cannot now pray to my Father, and He shall presently give me more than twelve legions of angels?" (26:53). In fact, Jesus' feelings had already been expressed by David, when he fled from Absalom, saying, "salvation belongeth unto the LORD; Thy blessing is upon Thy people. Selah" (Ps. 3:8). What Jesus said to Peter was not simply a matter of fact – Jesus did not need Peter's sword, as he had access to the care of a company of angels; the fact that Jesus could have called on so many angels to protect him indicates yet another test of Jesus' will power: this was a further temptation that Jesus had to resist.

Only a short while earlier in Gethsemane, Jesus' sweat had been like great drops of blood under the pressure of what he knew to be his Father's will for him. He had resolved that particular dilemma – my will or the Father's? – yet now he was presented with a further challenge. He only had to say the word and the angels would have come to his aid. But his mind was resolutely set. His question to Peter, "But how then shall the Scriptures be fulfilled, that thus it must be?" (Mt. 26:54), shows that Jesus knew, deep down, that there was no other way in which his Father's will could be fulfilled. He also understood that "to him that knoweth to do good, and doeth it not, to him it is sin" (Jas. 4:17) – not to yield to the Father's will would have been sinful for Jesus, and he would not fail at this last hurdle. Happily for us, Jesus was in full control of himself and resisted this additional possibility of failure. By contrast, the disciples were not in control, and they "all … forsook him, and fled" – we know not where (Mt. 26:56). And before we think any less of them for this, let us assess honestly how well (or otherwise!) we manage in our personal struggles at times of testing. And let us remember, too, that unlike Jesus, we "have not yet resisted unto blood, striving against sin" (Heb. 12:4).

They all forsook him and fled

What did the eleven do when they fled from Gethsemane? In fact, the record is almost silent about the movements of the disciples from the time that they fled up to the resurrection morning.

There is, however, at least some information about the movements of Peter and another disciple during the night when Jesus was arrested. Piecing the accounts together, we learn that when Jesus was taken to the high priest's house, "Simon Peter followed Jesus, and so did another disciple: that disciple was known unto the high priest, and went in with Jesus into the palace of the high priest" (Jno. 18:15). Part way through the evening proceedings Peter, having denied his Lord, "went out, and wept bitterly" (Lk. 22:62). Later, when Jesus was crucified, "there stood by the cross of Jesus his mother, and his mother's sister, Mary the wife of Cleophas, and Mary Magdalene" (Jno. 19:25); and in that dreadful situation, the mother of Jesus was entrusted to "the disciple standing by, whom he (Jesus) loved" (19:26), so we can conclude that one of the twelve was present during the crucifixion.

Although Peter followed Jesus "afar off" (Mk. 14:54) we should not think lightly of him. That Peter followed at all, rather than fleeing, advertises his love for his Master mingled with fear; but he had risked his life in striking off Malchus' ear. And he had said (and surely meant it): "I will lay down my life for thy sake" (Jno. 13:37). Jesus did not command the disciples to follow him into the city – all he had said about them was "let these go their way" (18:8); so the desire to be near to Jesus on the part of at least two of the disciples must be seen against the background of their initial flight from Gethsemane. Peter and the other disciple (probably John) must have decided together to go to the palace of the High Priest; and one of them (John) followed Jesus to the "place of a skull".

On the resurrection morning, Peter and John were together, since Mary Magdalene, on finding the tomb empty, ran and told Peter and "the other disciple, whom Jesus loved" (20:2). So we know that Peter and John were together on the resurrection morning – as they probably had been since the crucifixion, and Mary Magdalene knew where she would be able to find them. We know nothing of the movements of the other nine disciples who fled from Gethsemane, until after the resurrection.

These things were not done in a corner

As mentioned earlier, the whole of the environs of Jerusalem would be teeming with people, with families camping out on the slopes of the Mount of Olives. The large band of men who came to capture Jesus, "with lanterns and torches and weapons" (Jno. 18:3), will have been seen by many of those pilgrims. The return to the city, with Jesus "bound" (18:12), will not have gone unnoticed either. Many questions will have been rife among those who witnessed these events first-hand, and rumours must soon have spread throughout the city. Despite the concern of the chief priests to try to avoid an uproar among the common people (Mt. 26:5), the arrest of Jesus cannot have passed totally unnoticed.

Summary of the day before the Passover

- As in respect of the previous day, the Gospel writers provide little information about the events of the daytime activities of Jesus on the day before the Passover. We learn about the planning of the Passover meal in a location known to Jesus, but kept secret from all the other disciples except Peter and John.

- The evening meal in the upper room provides an insight into the way in which the disciples had failed to learn humility. They were still striving about who might be the greatest in the Kingdom after three and a half years with Jesus. His object lesson of washing their feet shows that actions can speak very powerfully.

- Jesus knew that this was to be the last time he would have opportunity to instruct his disciples before his death. He used that time to finish the instruction he had been giving all through his ministry. By their many questions, the disciples showed their inability to understand what Jesus was saying. By contrast, Jesus manifested his patience in the way that he took time to answer every question he was asked. He also prayed for Peter and the others because he knew what was to come and how they would be affected by the coming events.

- The behaviour of Judas in the upper room and beyond follows the pattern set on the previous evening, in Bethany, and shows him on his chosen, downward path, despite the Lord's strenuous efforts to pull him back from the brink of betrayal.

- There are so many links between the experiences of Jesus in these closing hours of his 'freedom' and those of his ancestor King David during Absalom's rebellion that it would be hard to imagine that Jesus was not sharing the feelings of his father David at various points during the evening. David's friend Ahithophel had turned against him and provided a prophetic pattern of the treacherous behaviour of Judas towards Jesus.

- As Jesus crossed the Brook Kidron with his disciples, he will undoubtedly have been reminded of David, as he fled from Absalom, passing over the same spot, "toward the way of the wilderness" (2 Sam. 15:23). Jesus, by contrast, "went forth … over the brook Cedron, where was a garden" (Jno. 18:1); and, as these are the only two occasions in Scripture where we read of someone crossing the Kidron, we are surely expected to note the contrast. David did not know what the outcome of his experiences would be, and he went from Kidron into a wilderness.

Jesus, by contrast, knowing the outcome, went into a garden. Because of Jesus' faithfulness, we too are not journeying towards a "wilderness" but rather to a garden – to Eden restored, where we will have right to the "tree of life" (Rev. 2:7).

- In Gethsemane, Jesus began at last to address his own needs; but, sadly, he gained no comfort from his sleeping disciples as he faced the greatest trial of his faith and wrestled with his natural wish not to die. He will have taken some comfort from his fervent prayers to his Father, and from his ancestor David's deliverance from the evil intentions of Absalom. David did not know the future. He did not know whether or not he would return to Jerusalem in peace. By contrast, Jesus knew that his faithfulness to his Father would bring the joy of divine approval. As the Psalmist puts it: "Thou wilt shew me the path of life: in Thy presence is fulness of joy; at Thy right hand there are pleasures for evermore" (Ps. 16:11).

Chapter 8:
Summing up: the highlights of the week

This has been a week packed with activity – a week that Jesus knew would end with his arrest and crucifixion: the entry into Jerusalem; confrontations on the temple mount; attempts by the religious leaders to discredit Jesus in the eyes of the people; two intimate meals; Jesus' last words to the religious leaders of his day; Jesus' prophetic words on the Mount of Olives; the last supper; Jesus' final words to his disciples as they crossed the city on their way towards the Garden of Gethsemane; Jesus' prayers to his Father in Gethsemane; his betrayal and arrest.

The combined instruction from the four Gospel narratives is "written for our learning" (Rom. 15:4), that our hope might be strengthened. We see the patience of the Lord throughout the week – first with the religious leaders: despite their open hostility towards him, he makes appeals to them for repentance. We see his patience with the twelve disciples who, despite continuing with him throughout his ministry. still struggled to understand many of the key things he was telling them.

One of the most helpful things we read about is the Last Supper – the memorial that Jesus established for our benefit as we reflect on his life of total obedience. And we are privileged to eavesdrop on his answers to the disciples' questions, hear his teachings as he crosses the Kidron, and listen in awe as he prays in solitude to his Father.

And perhaps the supreme encouragement we learn from the week is that, despite opposition, persecution and death, the promise of Emmanuel – 'God with us' – is as true for us as it was for the eleven who heard the promise of the Father and of His son dwelling with us.

Appendix 1:
A calendar of events

A summary of the last week of Jesus' life up to the Resurrection [1]

Days before and after the Feast		Events of the day	Day of month Nisan	Time of day	Jewish day of week	Gentile day of week	Day/Night
	6	Jesus arrives at Bethany to lodge	9	6pm	7th	Fri	
John 12:1		Weekly Sabbath	9	Evening 6am	7th	Fri	
		Weekly Sabbath	9	Morning Noon 6pm	7th	Sat	
John 12:2	5		10	Evening 6pm	1st	Sat	
Mark 11:1-11; John 12:12		Entry into Jerusalem Return	10	Morning Noon 6pm	1st	Sun	

1 This table is almost identical to a table printed in *The Christadelphian* in July 1996. The substance of the study which produced this table owes much to Brother John Dunning and the campaigners who worked on 'The last week of Jesus' life' in Monmouth, England during Easter Week in 1996.

	Days before and after the Feast	Events of the day	Day of month Nisan	Time of day	Jewish day of week	Gentile day of week	Day/Night
	4	To Bethany	11	Evening 6am	2nd	Sun	
Mark 11:12-19		Fig tree cursed Return	11	Morning Noon 6pm	2nd	Mon	
	3	To Bethany	12	Evening 6am	3rd	Mon	
Mark 11:20		Fig tree withered In the Temple Olivet Prophecy	12	Morning Noon 6pm	3rd	Tue	
Mark 14:1	2	Feast at Bethany	13	Evening 6am	4th	Tue	
Mark 14:12		Upper Room made ready	13	Morning Noon 6pm	4th	Wed	
	1	Last Supper Gethsemane Betrayal / Arrest	14	Evening 6am	5th	Wed	
John 19:31; Mark 15:34	Day of Preparation for Passover; A day of unleavened bread	Trial and Crucifixion Jesus dies & Passover Lamb killed	14	Morning Noon 3pm 6pm	5th	Thu	In the tomb
Lev. 23:6-7	Passover	Feast of Unleavened Bread Passover Sabbath	15	Evening 6am	6th	Thu	1

	Days before and after the Feast	Events of the day	Day of month Nisan	Time of day	Jewish day of week	Gentile day of week	Day/Night
John 19:31	First day	High day Passover Sabbath	15	Morning Noon 6pm	6th	Fri	1
		Weekly Sabbath	16	Evening 6am	7th	Fri	2
	Second day	Weekly Sabbath	16	Morning 6am	7th	Sat	2
		Resurrection	17	Evening 6am	1st	Sat	3
Lev. 23:11; Luke 24:21	Third day	of Jesus	17	Morning Noon 6pm	1st	Sun	3

Appendix 2:
Bible echoes: David's flight from Absalom

Old Testament themes

Whilst the Gospels provide a detailed account of the events of the last week of Jesus' life, we need to be alert to Bible echoes (from other Scriptures). By the careful use of language, the Spirit is pointing us to links with earlier Bible events. Such links might be considered tenuous if viewed in isolation; but given that they are used extensively and in detail at more than one point in the records of this last week, the existence of the links, and their force, becomes self-evident. Some of these links are tabulated here, having been discussed in detail at the relevant place in the study. The links are listed below in the order in which the particular 'echo' is first heard.

David's flight from Absalom

David and Absalom		Jesus	
Scripture	Event	Event	Scripture
2 Samuel 15:30	Ascent of Mount of Olives	Descent of Mount of Olives	Luke 19:37
2 Samuel 15:30	Followers with David	Disciples with Jesus	Luke 19:37

David and Absalom		Jesus	
Scripture	Event	Event	Scripture
2 Samuel 15:30	People weeping	People rejoicing	Luke 19:37
2 Samuel 15:14	"Smite with the edge of the sword"	"Fall by the edge of the sword"	Luke 21:24
Psalm 41:9	"He that eateth … lifted up his heel"		John 13:17
2 Samuel 15:23	David crossed the Kidron	Jesus crossed the Kidron	John 18:1
2 Samuel 16:6	Shimei was casting stones	"A stone's cast"	Luke 22:41
2 Samuel 15:26	"Let [God] do to me as seemeth good unto Him"	"Not my will but Thine be done"	Matthew 26:39; Mark 14:36; Luke 22:42
Psalm 69:20 [1]	"I looked for comforters and found none"	"Could ye not watch with me one hour?"	Matthew 26:40
2 Samuel 16:9	Abishai wanted to remove Shimei's head	Peter cut off Malchus' ear	Matthew 26:51; Mark 14:47; Luke 22:50; John 18:10
2 Samuel 17:23	Ahithophel hanged himself	Judas hanged himself	Matthew 27:5

---

1 Psalm 69 speaks of the rebellion of Absalom and the involvement of Ahithophel. Peter (Acts 1:20) quotes Psalm 69:25 and applies it to Judas along with Psalm 109:8 – another Psalm speaking about the same rebellion. Judas answers to Ahithophel in this context, and those Psalms which speak of Ahithophel also speak in anticipation of Judas. We might, therefore, reflect on the way that David felt about Ahithophel's treachery and the Lord's feelings about Judas. Whilst the New Testament gives no indication of Jesus' sadness at the behaviour of Judas, the Psalms show that the betrayal by Judas was a great personal disappointment to the Lord.

Appendix 3:
Bible echoes: The Olivet Prophecy

Echoes of the Olivet Prophecy

We have already alluded to the fact that Jesus warned the religious leaders about the destruction of the temple. In fact, he told them on two separate occasions during the final week that this terrible event was going to happen. The first occasion was as he was entering Jerusalem on the ass. As he approached the city, he lamented over it (Lk. 13:34). The second time was when he spoke his final words to the religious leaders, warning them that the desolation of their house was imminent (Mt. 23:37).

The use of Isaiah 8 in the Olivet Prophecy

Jesus has already used Isaiah 8 as a challenge to the religious leaders (Mt. 21:44). The Olivet Prophecy was spoken to warn and encourage the disciples. It speaks of the destruction of Herod's temple, which took place when the Romans sacked Jerusalem in AD 70. Isaiah 8 speaks of the forthcoming Assyrian invasion of Judah, and in particular the siege of Jerusalem in the days of Hezekiah. There are striking similarities between this and the siege of AD 70.

Hezekiah	Event	AD 70
The Assyrians	An occupying army close by	The Romans
Isaiah 8:8 – The Assyrians will "reach to the neck"	Impending destruction of the temple	Olivet Prophecy
Hezekiah	A righteous man calling for repentance	Jesus
Hezekiah leads a religious revival and saves the nation	The common people hearken to a righteous leader	Jesus welcomed as 'Saviour' by the crowd on his entry into Jerusalem
Isaiah 8:10	God with us	Jesus

There is also a cluster of words in the Olivet Prophecy quoted from Isaiah 8:

Isaiah 8:14	"snare"	Luke 21:35
Isaiah 8:15	"fall"	Luke 21:24
Isaiah 8:15	"taken"	Matthew 24:40

In quoting language from Isaiah 8, Jesus is drawing the attention of his hearers to the way in which Isaiah's words are going to be fulfilled again. However, there is a contrast between the days of Hezekiah and Jesus' days. In Hezekiah's days the destruction was averted through repentance. In the days of Hezekiah, Micah prophesied "Therefore shall Zion for your sake be plowed as a field, and Jerusalem shall become heaps, and the mountain of the house as the high places of the forest" (Mic. 3:12). This message from the prophet brought about repentance:

"Micah the Morasthite prophesied in the days of Hezekiah king of Judah, and spake to all the people of Judah, saying, Thus saith the LORD of hosts; Zion shall be plowed like a field, and Jerusalem shall become heaps, and the mountain of the house as the high places of a forest. Did Hezekiah king of Judah and all Judah put him at all to death? did he not fear the LORD, and besought the LORD, and the LORD repented Him of the evil which He had pronounced against them?" (Jer. 26:18-19)

There would be no repentance in the first century: this time, therefore, Jerusalem and the temple would be destroyed.

Scripture index